GARDENING CAN BE MURDER

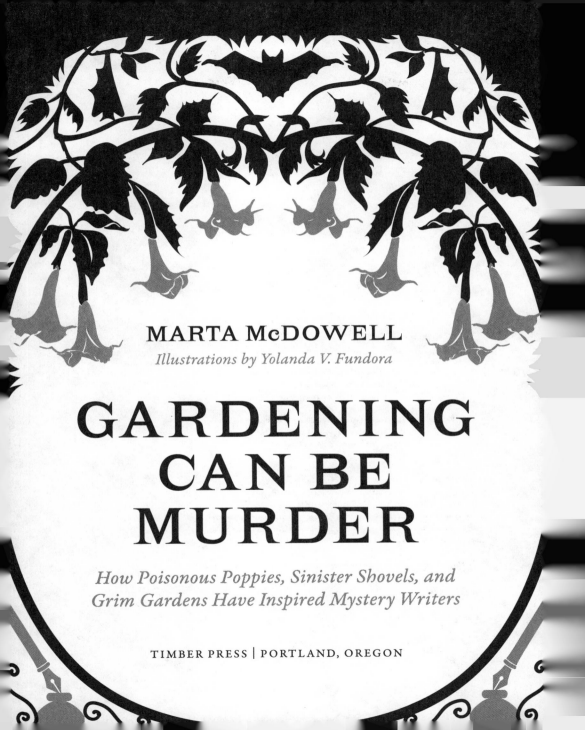

MARTA McDOWELL

Illustrations by Yolanda V. Fundora

GARDENING CAN BE MURDER

How Poisonous Poppies, Sinister Shovels, and Grim Gardens Have Inspired Mystery Writers

TIMBER PRESS | PORTLAND, OREGON

Published in 2023 by Timber Press, Inc. a subsidiary of Workman Publishing Co.,
a subsidiary of Hachette Book Group, Inc.
1290 Avenue of the Americas
New York, New York 10104
timberpress.com

Printed in the USA on responsibly sourced paper.
Text and cover design by Lauren Michelle Smith
Cover illustration sourced from Biodiversity Heritage Library/ *The instructive picture book*, or,
Lessons for the vegetable world by Charlotte M. Yonge, Plate XX Deadly Nightshade
The publisher is not responsible for websites (or their content) that are not owned by the publisher.

The Hachette Speakers Bureau provides a wide range of authors for speaking events. To find out
more, go to hachettespeakersbureau.com or email HachetteSpeakers@hbgusa.com.

ISBN 978-1-64326-112-6

Catalog records for this book are available from the Library of Congress and the British Library.

TO KIRKE, MY PERENNIAL
PARTNER IN CRIME

The door slammed behind her. Someone else had stepped into the room while she had been rummaging in the desk. Had they seen her? She dropped down and made herself as small as possible and hoped that

Gardening is not a rational act.

—MARGARET ATWOOD, "UNEARTHING SUITE"

*The vicar may have had a morbid fancy for something else—
a passion à la Plato for an aspidistra, or a strange, covetous
longing for a cactus. He's a great gardener, you know, and these
vegetable and mineral loves can be very sinister indeed.*

—DOROTHY L. SAYERS, *BUSMAN'S HONEYMOON*

*It was ridiculous to start sidelines like amateur
detection when you had a garden on your hands.*

—SHEILA PIM, *COMMON OR GARDEN CRIME*

*What lethal drops could be distilled from the entries at the
Spring Flower Show; what a jolly poison could be extracted from the
jonquil and what deadly liquors from the daffodil. Even
the common churchyard yew, so loved by poets and by courting couples,
contained within its seeds and leaves enough taxine
to put paid to half the population of England.*

—ALAN BRADLEY, *THE SWEETNESS AT THE BOTTOM OF THE PIE*

CONTENTS

INTRODUCTION

What is it about the garden that suits it to murder? Plants, plantings, and various horticultural paraphernalia make frequent appearances in mysteries, whether detective fiction or the more generic crime or gothic. Perhaps it is the gardener's natural malice toward weeds, rodents, and other garden undesirables. Rare is the gardener who can approach a slug without homicidal intent. Or perhaps it is the mythic struggle between good and evil, first played out with Eden's slithering snake against a garden backdrop. Let's face it, gardening can be murder.

My love of murder mysteries hatched early. It began with selections from my siblings' bookshelves—being last-born has its advantages. There were *Hardy Boys*, courtesy of my brother Jerry, alongside the yellow-and-black spines of *Nancy Drew* from Patty and Kay. In the low, brick building that housed the public library in our northern New Jersey suburb, *The Black Stallion Mystery* was a favorite. I read it over and over again.

When I graduated from the children's room to the grown-up side of the Chatham Library, I discovered the many titles of Phyllis A. Whitney. These were gothic mysteries, dripping with suspense and romance, punctuated by cliffhangers. At the time, the fact eluded me that Whitney's *The Moonflower* referred to the climbing *Ipomea alba*, although both the plant and the Japanese-style gardens that showcase it were prominent in the plot. Nor was I aware that the author's middle initial "A" stood for "Ayame," the Japanese word for "iris," a hint she had been born and raised in Japan. When I exhausted her titles, I segued to Mary Stewart and Daphne du Maurier, thence to Agatha Christie and beyond. The gore and glory of the public library's mystery section along with PBS, Acorn TV, BritBox, and Hallmark Mysteries have sustained my habit ever since. With the mystery genre booming in print and on screen at present, I have had no problem satisfying my cravings for crime.

Reading mysteries predated my gardening fixation by decades. It wasn't until my zigzag path to garden writing landed me with editor David Wheeler and his superb journal *Hortus* that detective fiction and horticulture dovetailed for me. My article, "With *Malus* Aforethought," appeared in the Spring 2002 issue. (*Malus* is the botanical name for apples, among others.) The idea for this book germinated from that seed.

This survey of the mystery genre and its horticultural connections—the poisoned pen and the trowel—is by no means exhaustive. It is limited to fiction available in English, due to my own language limitations. Within that, detective, suspense, and crime fiction abound, though avid readers of same may note with horror the omission of some favorite authors or titles. For that offense, I plead guilty, having followed my own preferences.

The structure of the classic murder mystery—detective, setting, motive, means, clues, suspects—provides the arc for this book. As connections between pen and trowel have long been my pursuit, I have added gardening profiles for a small sampling of mystery writers. One caveat: I've done my best to not spoil the plots for those who haven't read my selections, but, on occasion, hints couldn't be helped. Read on at your own risk.

Like most mysteries, those of the garden variety call for a minimum of one sleuth. Criminal investigation, whether vocation or avocation, calls for many of the same skills as horticulture.

A gardener, like a detective, needs to be observant. How did those holes get in the hosta leaves? As Sherlock Holmes once told Doctor Watson, "There is nothing more deceptive than an obvious fact." One collects pertinent evidence—a slime trail perhaps, or damage to other plants. Critical thinking is required. While the usual suspects for hosta mutilation would be a gang of slugs, it also might have been hailstones from last night's freak thunderstorm.

Is there justice in the garden? Not always. A sad truth is that once the verdict is in on a plant problem, there may not be a practical or ecologically sound way to fix it. Those bright red beetles that appear to disfigure the strappy leaves of my lilies will come back every year despite my best efforts. Closure is one of the more reliable comforts of the mystery genre; in most cases, a solution is revealed and appropriate punishment meted out.

There have always been mysteries in and out of the garden, but modern detecting, detective fiction, even the word "detective" are recent inventions, products of the later years of the Industrial Revolution. Even further back on the mystery timeline is the

Gothic novel. Like today's slasher films and horror fiction, the novels of Ann Radcliffe and her imitators appealed to the imaginative populace of late eighteenth-century Europe and America. The allure of "terror upon terror" drove sales of titles like *The Castle of Otranto*, *The Mysteries of Udolpho*, and the still-popular *Frankenstein*.

By the mid-nineteenth century, Edgar Allan Poe opened the door to modern crime fiction with a short story set in Paris. "Murders in the Rue Morgue," published in the April 1841 issue of *Graham's Magazine*, is credited with being the first modern murder mystery; its protagonist, Chevalier C. Auguste Dupin, was the first fictional detective. The remarkable, analytical Dupin was not a gardener however, and though the *Jardin des Plantes* shows up at the story's conclusion, that is due more to its animal menagerie than to its botanical riches. Poe's "Rue Morgue" is an urban tale of Parisian streets, alleys, and tall *maisons de ville*.

It was no accident that Poe chose Paris and a Parisian detective for his story. Reformed French criminal Eugène François Vidocq invented the profession of criminal investigation in the first years of the nineteenth century. He recruited and trained a select band of agents—mostly other ex-criminals—to assist uniformed officers in their work. In 1812, the Prefecture of Police in Paris designated his plainclothes brigade "the *Sûreté*." The

Edgar Allan Poe (1809–1849).

Sûreté became the prototype for Scotland Yard and later the FBI.

In fiction, Vidocq inspired his own lineup of detectives: Vautrin in Balzac's *Le Père Goriot* and Javert in Victor Hugo's *Les Miserables* (though confusingly, its hero, Jean Valjean, was also partly based on Vidocq). To the character Monsieur Dupin, Poe had added a new, differentiating trait. His detective solved crimes through the application of observation and reasoning—deduction—and a new genre was born.

In 1865, Emile Gaboriau followed Poe's lead with *L'Affaire Lerouge* (*The Lerouge Case*). Considered the first full-length detective novel, Gaboriau's book features, among others, an investigator named Lecoq—also inspired by Vidocq—with an older, wiser amateur sidekick named Monsieur Taberet. Lecoq would appear in four more of Gaboriau's novels and several short stories. While *L'Affaire Lerouge* is a village affair, garden references are scarce.

Meanwhile, publishers in Great Britain were fulfilling the demand of a literate and often commuting working class with popular penny fiction. These pulp booklets, precursors to pocket paperbacks, recounted tales of the macabre and the criminal. They are more gothic than crime fiction. Sweeney Todd, the "Demon Barber of Fleet Street" is one memorable example. No gardens there.

The "penny dreadfuls" lacked characters with that deductive frame of mind. But when the full-length detective novel crossed the Channel from France to England, the mystery decamped to the country and stepped, with its investigator, into the garden.

GARDENING DETECTIVES

Classic to Contemporary

Gardening detectives, both professional and amateur, abound in crime fiction and they appeared early on. Wilkie Collins introduced the first horticulturally inclined investigator in *The Moonstone*. The serialized story first appeared in the United Kingdom in January 1868 in Charles Dickens's periodical *All the Year Round* and simultaneously in *Harper's Weekly* in the United States. That summer, it also appeared as a "triple-decker," a three-volume set published by Tinsley Brothers in London. Unlike the cheap penny dreadfuls that had preceded it, the trio of hardcover books legitimized detective fiction in the English language. Dickens was a friend and mentor of Collins, and likely influenced him with his own Inspector Bucket, an intelligent, intuitive character who had appeared in *Bleak House* more than a decade earlier. But it is Collins who first gave his detective vital gardening credentials.

SERGEANT CUFF

One of these days (please God), I shall retire from catching thieves, and try my hand at growing roses.

SERGEANT CUFF IN *THE MOONSTONE* (1868)

Unlike Poe's Auguste Dupin, Sergeant Cuff is a professional crime fighter, an inspector at the Metropolitan Branch, now famously known as Scotland Yard. We never learn his first name. Cuff is often heard whistling "The Last Rose of Summer," an immensely popular if mournful song by Irish poet Thomas Moore, set to a traditional air. (If you aren't familiar with the song, the version recorded by Nina Simone is superb.) Wilkie Collins omitted the lyrics from the book. Why bother when every nineteenth century reader would have known them by heart? It is a gardener's lament, and a lover's:

> 'Tis the last rose of summer,
> Left blooming alone;
> All her lovely companions
> Are faded and gone;
> No flower of her kindred,
> No rose-bud is nigh,
> To reflect back her blushes
> Or give sigh for sigh!
>
> I'll not leave thee, thou lone one,
> To pine on the stem;
> Since the lovely are sleeping,

> Go, sleep thou with them.
>   Thus kindly I scatter
>   Thy leaves o'er the bed
>   Where thy mates of the garden
>   Lie scentless and dead.
>
> So soon may I follow,
>   When friendships decay,
>   And from love's shining circle
>   The gems drop away!
>   When true hearts lie withered,
>   And fond ones are flown,
>   Oh! who would inhabit
>   This bleak world alone?

The words fit hand-in-glove with the plot. Or perhaps jewel-in-setting would be a better analogy. *The Moonstone* revolves around a sacred diamond, looted by an officer of the British East India Company at the storming of Seringapatam—a fictional gem, but a real battle that took place in southern India on the fourth of May 1799. There is reason to believe the diamond is cursed. In the novel, the valuable jewel makes its way to London and thence to the Yorkshire estate of the widowed Lady Verinder as a bequest to—or, one might say, a hex on—her daughter. It is eighteen-year-old Rachel Verinder's birthday. That night after receiving her gift, the diamond disappears.

Sergeant Cuff is called to the scene. Rachel's cousin Franklin Blake declares, "If half the stories I have heard are true, when it comes to unravelling a mystery, there isn't an equal in England of Sergeant Cuff." The gaunt, grey-haired Cuff has, we are told, a face "as sharp as a hatchet" with skin "as yellow and withered as an autumn leaf." In his black suit and white cravat, he could be a cleric or an undertaker. One would not have taken him for a gardener, yet a gardener he is. "When I *have* a moment's fondness to bestow, most times the roses get it," says Cuff.

Plant lovers can be split into two families. Generalists have rarely met a green growing thing they didn't like and, more often than not, want to bring home to their own gardens. I count myself among their number. Then there are the specialists. A particular plant captures the specialist's heart. It might be the Rose, Dahlia, or African Violet, though sometimes it is a broader grouping like alpines or native plants. Out of this fervor, plant societies and exhibitions are born.

For Sergeant Cuff, there is only one plant: the rose. While he mentions, with modesty, that he hopes to try his hand at growing them, he is already something of an authority. Through his eyes and exclamations, the reader steps into the Verinder rose garden, entered through an evergreen arch and laid out as a circle in a square. There are blush roses and musk, and the "old English rose holding up its head along with the best and the newest of them." He approves of the orientation, with "the right exposure to the south and sou'-west." While collecting clues and drawing inferences in the mystery of the Moonstone, he finds time to engage Lady Verinder's gardener in intense rose-related debates, including the relative merits of grass versus gravel for surfacing rose garden walks.

Lady Verinder's "rosery" and Sergeant Cuff's passion reflect the horticultural trend of the day. The nineteenth century was a boom time for rose growing in England. While roses have a long history in the British Isles, they had a slow start. A mere handful of species and hybrids grew in the villas of the Roman occupiers, the walled gardens of medieval castle and monastery, and the physic gardens and manicured beds of the early modern era. The War of the Roses gave two of them—a white rose and a

" 'One of these days (please God) I shall retire from catching thieves, and try my
hand at growing roses.' "—p. 90.

Wilkie Collins (1824–1889).

red—bloody notoriety; the Tudors adopted a third. But the introduction of the China rose, *Rosa chinensis*, to Europe in the mid-1700s tipped the scale. Enthusiastic hybridizers on both sides of the Channel and across the Atlantic began crossing china roses with other known varieties. Results were spectacular. The offspring yielded a spectrum of color, fragrance, and habit as well as a tendency to rebloom in one season. By the reign of Victoria, a rose garden was a must, whether you were one of the landed gentry like Lady Verinder or stood solidly with Sergeant Cuff in the echelons of the respectable working class.

Through the course of the story, we find Sergeant Cuff and Verinder's Scottish gardener, Mr. Begbie, wrangling over the grafting of roses. The arguments were friendly, if intense, sometimes lubricated by a bottle of whiskey. Would the white moss rose be more likely to flourish on the roots of a dog rose? "Yes," says Begbie; "No," says Cuff, it should be grown on its own roots. Grafting the canes of a tender rose onto hardier root stock of a different species can increase its vigor. Their argument evokes the novel's themes of race and empire. It parallels the love triangle propelling *The Moonstone*.

Rachel Verinder, the daughter of the house, seems to be falling for the passionate if directionless Franklin Blake, who is recently back from years on the Continent. Competing for her affections is the well-known, seemingly bland philanthropist Godfrey Ablewhite. Which gentleman would be the more appropriate match? And what is the connection to rose grafting?

Gardeners were well acquainted with the native dog rose, *Rosa canina*, a familiar plant of hedgerow and scrubland. Samuel Reynolds Hole, a prominent rosarian of the time, called it "the jolly Dog-Rose, that rough, wild vagabond." He wondered about the propriety of its union with more refined species like the white moss rose. S. Reynolds Hole might as well have been comparing rough, wild Franklin Blake to the polished Ablewhite.

The Reverend Hole, an Anglican priest and later Dean of Rochester Cathedral, was a personality in his own right. He had long cultivated a garden at the vicarage in Caunton Manor, but with nary a rose within. His first encounter with roses was a sort of "road to Damascus" event. He'd been asked to judge an Easter Monday rose exhibition, put on by a local working men's club in nearby Nottingham. With the fragrant, blooming entries displayed in an upstairs room of a corner pub, he was converted. Hole went on to organize England's first national show dedicated to the genus, held in London in 1858. It became an annual event and promulgated rose growing in fact and fiction.

Wilkie Collins, a Londoner, was so familiar with the city's floral exhibitions, he wrote them into *The Moonstone*. When Rachel, distressed by the loss of her diamond, moves to the family's residence in town, she takes up a "whole round of gaieties." There are operas, balls, and "flower-shows." Roses bloom throughout the plot. They fill the window of the Verinders' London sitting room and adorn gentlemen's buttonholes. They sidle into the name of a desolate servant, Rosanna Spearman, who is a key to the action. Yet despite this rosy window dressing, the disappearance of the Moonstone continues to nag at all—even, it seems, the retired Sergeant Cuff.

Gardening had always been Cuff's retirement plan, a plan he implements as the story progresses. When the case stalls, Lady Verinder dismisses him, and he trades Scotland Yard for a small "yard" of his own in Surrey, south of London. When Franklin Blake, one of the many suspects, makes his way to Cuff's rural cottage, he notes:

Through the trellis-work, ... [I] saw the great Cuff's favorite flower everywhere; blooming in his garden, clustering over his door, looking in at windows. Far from the crimes and the mysteries of the great city, the illustrious thief-taker was placidly living out the last Sybarite years of his life, smothered in roses!

Cuff is not at home to receive his caller but off on a trip to Ireland, visiting some "great man's gardener [who] has found out something new in the growing of roses." The former detective has turned his analytical skills and prodigious energy to "the peaceful floricultural attractions of a country life" and the full-time pursuit of the genus *Rosa*. Without giving away the denouement, suffice it to say that Cuff suspends his retirement, the diamond returns to its rightful place, and wedding bells ring. We can presume that Cuff happily returned to Surrey to live out his life among the roses.

MISS JANE MARPLE

Gardening is good as a smoke-screen, and the habit of observing birds through powerful glasses can always be turned to account.

—MISS MARPLE IN *MURDER AT THE VICARAGE* (1930)

Sergeant Cuff, groundbreaker of gardening detectives in English language mysteries, was followed by a host of compatriots. Had he visited Agatha Christie's Miss Marple in her fictional village of St. Mary Mead, assuredly they would have discussed roses. In December 1927, Christie unveiled Jane Marple in a set of short stories, delicious to read, with glimpses into a character still developing in the mind of her creator.

Marple's first mention is as Aunt Jane. Her nephew Raymond West, a writer, describes her in detail. The genteel Miss Marple wears old-fashioned attire. That evening her dress was brocade and lace; in later stories it would often be tweed. Her posture is impeccable, her hair white, her blue eyes faded but alert. Seated in her comfortable parlor, her hands are busy with knitting needles and wool.

Raymond addresses a small group that he has assembled for a "Tuesday Night Club." Joining him and his aunt, we have an artist, a clergyman, a solicitor, and a retired commissioner of Scotland Yard. Their purpose is to reconsider unsolved mysteries, what today we would call cold cases. Aunt Jane may flutter and digress, but at the conclusion of each short story she proves the canniest of the bunch.

She also proves an avid gardener. The character quickly emerged as one of Christie's favorite detectives. Miss Marple's first book-length appearance, *Murder at the Vicarage* (1930), offers more detail about her place in the wider world as well as the world of horticulture.

Her gardens surround a comfortable house that faces the High Street in the prototypical English village of St. Mary Mead. Set well back from the road, her snug property sits between Dr. Haydock's—the local medical practitioner—on one side and Miss Hartnell's on the other. A little lane runs diagonally behind her back garden and terminates at the vicar's garden gate. Neighbors walking down the lane are well positioned to admire Miss Marple's roses, and she is equally well positioned to observe the goings-on.

A public footpath opposite her back gate runs through a woodland, the perfect spot for an illicit rendezvous or for sequestering a clue. In *Murder at the Vicarage*, we encounter one of the suspects exploring the woods, looking for a nice rock for Miss Marple's garden—not just any garden, but her *Japanese* garden.

In real-life London, they were all the rage. The Japan-British Exhibition of 1910 had set it off. A giant trade fair, the Exhibition's 140-acre site included two large gardens: the Garden of Floating Islands and the Garden of Peace. (The latter has been reconstructed in Hammersmith

Park.) Japanese specialists designed the two show gardens; a Japanese head gardener supervised their construction. There were tea houses and temples, specimen plants from Japan, naturalistic water features and, of course, many rocks.

Held in the Great White City in Shepherd's Bush, the Exhibition's six-month run from May through October 1910 attracted eight million visitors. It isn't a stretch to think that a twenty-year-old Miss Agatha Miller—before she married Archibald Christie in 1914—attended the Exhibition, as she often stayed with her paternal grandmother in London. The craze for Japanese gardens came to an abrupt halt when Japan allied with Germany and Italy in 1940 during the Second World War.

As Miss Marple emerged fully mature from Christie's typewriter over the course of twenty short stories and twelve novels, many details came to light about her gardening interests, though not precisely how and when she acquired her horticultural skills. A German governess taught Jane and her sister about the language of flowers, knowledge which later proves valuable in deciphering clues. Jane Marple prefers antique roses over the newer hybrids. Her garden is filled with the fragrant flowers of an English cottage garden. There are peonies and sweet peas. Of heliotropes, she knows that the cultivar 'Cherry Pie' is prized for its scent.

Miss Marple is knowledgeable on all subjects horticultural. When called upon, she can name a plant with proper nomenclature. With a detective's eye, she identifies white-flowering silver fleece vine as *Polygonum baldschuanicum*. (I like to think she would also know it has since been reclassified as *Fallopia aubertii*.) By whatever alias, she recognizes the plant as a menace, growing at a terrifying rate and spreading by seed and underground runners.

As to garden maintenance, Marple has high standards. Weeds vex her, whether in her own garden or elsewhere. Groundsel and ground elder are among her archenemies. She reserves her harshest words for bindweed, the worst fiend of all. Like some murders, it has long, insidious roots. Poorly pruned shrubs make her long for her secateurs. She keeps her roses deadheaded to prolong their bloom. Slugs are a worry. The garden means hard work to Miss Marple, but also great pleasure, a balance that any avid gardener can appreciate.

She has friends who share her gardening enthusiasm. Prominent among them is Dolly Bantry, whose passion and budget for plants exceed her own. Dolly's favorite reading material is a bulb catalogue. One generally finds her with fingers in the soil working in the flower gardens at her home, Gossington Hall. Dolly and her friend Jane commiserate over the lack of rain. (Gardeners, fictional and otherwise, are notable complainers about the weather.) Dolly is careful with her gentians, proud of her delphiniums, and boastful of her irises. Though Dolly has many sterling qualities, humility is not among them.

Reading mystery series that endure for decades sometimes requires a healthy suspension of disbelief on the part of devoted fans. If, as Christie once said, Miss Marple was born at age sixty-five or seventy, she must have been upward of one hundred and ten by the end of her run. Dame Agatha, honored by Queen Elizabeth in 1971, remained silent on her character's birthdays as time went on. But in *The Mirror Crack'd from Side to Side* (1962), Christie has Miss Marple confront some realities about the passage of time for a garden and a gardener.

Getting old is inevitable. For a gardener it is an especially bitter pill. Miss Marple's doctor has forbidden most horticultural tasks. Her days of planting and digging are over; only light pruning is permitted. The gardener she employs is disappointing. "Old Laycock" comes like clockwork three times a week but has more enthusiasm for consuming cups of tea and cultivating vegetables and annuals than for maintaining Miss Marple's herbaceous border. Her lovely canterbury bells have been replaced with pedestrian salvias. He chops her heirloom rosebushes as if they were hybrid teas, and he hasn't the least interest in trenching her sweet peas or coddling the meconopsis.

Her friend Dolly, a contemporary in age, is also forced to give up her mammoth gardening endeavors. By the time of *The Mirror Crack'd*, the now-widowed Dolly Bantry has downsized. She has sold Gossington Hall. When she isn't abroad, she lives in the East Lodge on the only corner of the property she retained. The new owners of the Hall, a film star and her producer husband, are opening the house and grounds—now maintained by an outside firm and enhanced with a swimming pool—for a charity benefit. Dolly eagerly attends. If one can no longer tend one's own borders, one can still engage vicariously by visiting other people's gardens and discussing the changes—tsk, tsk—with one's best friend.

Miss Marple's final case was *Nemesis*, published in 1971. (Though the publisher advertised *Sleeping Murder* [1976] as "Miss Marple's Last Case," Christie had written it in the 1940s and banked the manuscript for her heirs who published it after her death.) In *Nemesis*, Miss Marple is unequivocal in terms of garden preferences. It is flowers over vegetables for her, as it was for Agatha Christie, choosing aesthetic over utilitarian in the garden. Yet we find evidence that Jane Marple made some exceptions for herbs and other useful plants.

Through the course of the novels and short stories, Miss Marple offers a variety of home-brewed garden tonics. A soporific infusion of chamomile would soothe a restless guest. Tansy is a key ingredient in her grandmother's herbal tea. She steeps macerated plums in sugar and alcohol for her special damson gin. *Primula veris*, the basis for her cowslip wine, blooms wild in the fields and meadows around the village. That is fortunate, as every batch needs several pecks of bloom.

Among sleuths, Miss Marple has good company in her interest in botanicals of the homeopathic and alcoholic varieties, including a medieval monk gardening at an abbey near the Welsh border.

BROTHER CADFAEL

They had entered the walled garden, and were suddenly
engulfed and drowned in all those sun-drenched fragrances, rosemary,
thyme, fennel, dill, sage, lavender, a whole world
of secret sweetness. The heat of the sun lingered, heady with
scent, even into the cool of the evening. Over their heads
swifts wheeled and screamed in ecstasy.

—**BROTHER CADFAEL IN *ONE CORPSE TOO MANY* (1980)**

Eight centuries before Miss Marple, another gardener-sleuth in the British Isles tended a fictional herb garden. Brother Cadfael is a creation of Ellis Peters, one of several *noms de plume* of British author Edith Pargeter, who penned dozens of novels between the thirties and the nineties, with twenty of them featuring her well known detective of the cloth. Cadfael is an early twelfth-century Welsh monk, and the herbalist of the Benedictine Abbey of Saint Peter and Saint Paul in Shrewsbury. Of middle years, Cadfael was blessed with a late vocation after wide experience with warfare, women, and life in general.

Ellis Peters popularized a subgenre, the historical mystery, layering the patina of the distant past with the established formula of the whodunnit. As with Miss Marple, Cadfael's chronicles can be pegged to events from the historical record. A delegation headed by Prior Robert from Shrewsbury did, in fact, "translate" the bones of St. Winifred from Holywell in Wales to the Abbey church in 1138. The period of civil strife that appears in the foreground of many of the Cadfael plots was so bloody and prolonged that historians have dubbed it "The Anarchy." Accounts of church and state provided Ellis Peters with perfect backdrops for murder. The Benedictine monastic practices gave her a solid motive for placing her protagonist in a garden.

The Rule of Saint Benedict was old by Cadfael's day. Written by Benedict of Nursia in the sixth century, it laid out the ideal practices for a religious community with a central tenet of *ora et labora*—prayer and work—alongside the usual triumvirate of poverty, chastity, and obedience. The concept of work as integral to monastic life, linked with Benedict's dictates for treatment of guests and care of the sick, elevated the importance of the medicinal garden. This garden was Cadfael's domain.

Unlike Miss Marple's St. Mary Mead, it is possible to find Shrewsbury on maps of England. It is in the county of Shropshire immediately to the east of the border with Wales. Shrewsbury Abbey still sits on the main road near the river Severn, not far from the English Bridge and south of the castle. But should you attempt a pilgrimage to seek out the monastery's herb garden, blame your disappointment on Henry VIII's sticky divorce and the monastic dissolution in its aftermath.

The Abbey, founded in 1083, was disbanded by the king's henchpersons in January 1540, and the abbot and monks pensioned off. St. Winifred's bones were scattered to the gale force of the Reformation. The Abbey's precincts were destroyed. There are some remnants: a few walls and the refectory pulpit. Parts of the eleventh-century nave and transept are incorporated into the much-restored Abbey church, now a part of the Church of England's Diocese of Lichfield. All traces have vanished of cloister garth, herb and vegetable gardens, and orchard. We must instead rely on the careful interpretation and creative power of Ellis Peters to see them through the day-to-day life of her main character.

As the Abbey's herbalist, Brother Cadfael is most often busy in the herb garden or in the adjacent workshop for drying, storing, and extracting essences from the harvest. He is a skilled gardener, curious in the old Latin sense of the word, as in *cura* for "care" and *curiosus* for "careful." The equivalent of today's pharmacist, he takes pains over plants and people, making tinctures and salves, draughts and syrups.

When we meet him in the first novel of the series, *A Morbid Taste for Bones*, he has been responsible for the abbey's herb garden for over a decade. The twenty books that follow find him thinning seedlings, enriching the garden soil, hybridizing poppies, and planting crops in rotation and succession. Where he learned to distinguish willowherb from thyme is unknown, though it may have been in his wanderings around the Mediterranean, first as a crusader who made his way to Jerusalem and later as a sea captain.

Cadfael is equally curious about unusual occurrences—particularly deaths—that take place in and around the abbey. (While a religious house seems an incongruous place for multiple homicides, it is an unfortunate fact that settings for mystery series are, by definition, murder magnets.) Plants offer hints to Cadfael, clues about where or how a particular person has died, a medieval foretaste of modern forensics.

Cadfael's garden is typical of the Norman period. While Ellis Peters did not tend her own herb garden—she once told an interviewer from *Mother Earth Living* that the plants in her garden that would qualify as herbs were limited to a few kitchen standbys like rosemary—she was a meticulous researcher. A careful read of the Cadfael series is an entertaining, informative introduction to the layout and plantings of the monastery's gardens.

Cadfael's herb garden at Shrewsbury Abbey is walled, a *hortus conclusus*. His faith honors the symbolism of the enclosed garden: the purity of the Virgin, the Annunciation, the new Jerusalem, and the bond of savior and church. But Cadfael the gardener appreciates its masonry walls for their functionality. They keep out animals for one. As important, they concentrate and retain the heat embraced by the many exotic plants Cadfael has assembled. He grows poppies, for example, from *paynim* seeds collected in his travels (*paynim* being the Middle English word for "pagan" or, at the time, "Muslim"). Nowadays we know them as *Papaver somniferum*, or opium poppies.

Five of the Cadfael books, plus a short story called "A Rare Benedictine," refer to the healing powers of lavender. The lavender in the Abbey's walled garden, also native to the Mediterranean, was common in monastery gardens throughout Europe by Cadfael's time. The Benedictine abbess Hildegard of Bingen, a contemporary of the fictional Cadfael, wrote of healing plants in her *Physica*, in the 1150s. Of lavender she recommended the following, here translated from the original Latin:

> Spike lavender (spica) is hot and dry, and its heat is healthy. Whoever cooks this lavender in wine or, if he has no wine, honey and water, and frequently drinks it when it is warm, will lessen the pain in his liver and lungs, and the stuffiness in his chest. It also makes his thinking and disposition pure.

I like to picture the fictional Cadfael corresponding with the real Hildegard over the healing properties of plants such as lavender. However, Ellis Peters relied not on Hildegard's *Physica*, but on the herbal of another physician-botanist for her background research. "I draw a great deal on Culpeper," she said in a 1993 interview. "He's a much later period, of course, but his information is sound." Nicholas Culpeper was a seventeenth-century London physician, a profession which, at the time, combined doctor, apothecary, astrologist, and, in his case, renegade. An educated man of simple Puritan dress and an enthusiastic handlebar moustache, he took the radical step of writing a layman's manual of herbal cures in English rather than Latin. This self-help guide to healing, *The English Physician of 1652*, did not make him popular with his fellow medical practitioners, who saw it as undermining their authority—and income.

Throughout the Cadfael series, Peters referenced over one hundred plants. Among them was only one member of the orchid family, the wild English orchis that Brother Cadfael called fox-stones. (Why fox-stones? *Orchis mascula*, sometimes called the male orchid, has two dangling root tubers, suggesting to some the testicles of a male fox. Of this orchis, Culpeper wrote "under the dominion of Dame Venus...[they] provoke lust exceedingly.") But it would take another writer and his famous fictional detective, operating in the twentieth century rather than the twelfth, to bring orchids to prominence in the world of the mystery.

NERO WOLFE

Everything in life must have a purpose
except the culture of Orchidaceae.

—NERO WOLFE IN *FER-DE-LANCE* (1934)

Another detective who led a gardening lifestyle that might be considered, in some respects, monastic is Nero Wolfe, hero of the prolific writer Rex Stout. On opening the pages of any of the Nero Wolfe canon—over forty novels and almost as many short stories—we find his character in New York City, cloistered and content in his West 35th Street home. The eccentric, corpulent, and complicated Wolfe has a gourmet chef-in-residence, adding to his creature comforts. His ability to gather the information necessary for crime-solving—his principal source of income—is enabled by another member of staff: his ironic sidekick-narrator, Archie Goodwin. In the ample brownstone Wolfe remains, except under the most unusual circumstances. There he spends much of his time nurturing his beloved orchids.

If you climb the seven steps up from the sidewalk and gain admittance to Chez Wolfe, you won't see potted orchids in the public spaces. Should you snoop around the first floor, you may find some select cut blooms in Wolfe's office, but he guards most of his prized plants jealously. To see the ten-thousand-odd specimens would require an invitation to the plant rooms. You could take the stairs or, like Wolfe, summon the brownstone's 4-by-6 elevator.

His plant rooms form the fifth-floor penthouse. Wolfe started his orchid empire atop the building's roof when a passing fancy morphed into a something akin to madness. There are three glass rooms distinguished by the temperature requirements of different orchid species: cool, intermediate, and tropical. The rooms are outfitted with concrete benches and metal staging platforms (a kind of portable shelving) to facilitate display and air circulation. In the heat of summer, lath screens cover the glass to cut the intensity of the New York sun. There are smaller areas for propagation, potting, and storage. There is also a room or rooms—accommodations for the resident orchid expert, Theodore Horstmann. Archie describes him as "the best orchid nurse alive."

Horstmann assists Wolfe—or vice versa, depending on whom you ask—in cultivating the collection. Though the Nero Wolfe corpus reveals little about Horstmann's back-story—where he trained or worked prior to Wolfe's plant rooms is left unsaid—we do know that he has strong opinions on the finer points of cultivation and hybridization. The two do not always see eye-to-eye on these matters, and are sometimes heard in vociferous argument. It was the laconic Horstmann who designed the misting equipment that maintains proper humidity. Archie, among his many responsibilities, keeps the detailed orchid inventory—acquisitions, breeding records, and the occasional demise of a plant—in the first-floor office that he shares with his boss.

Author Rex Stout, in a 1963 article in *Life Magazine*, recounted the origin story of his character's obsession. "Wolfe started on orchids many years ago with a specimen plant of *Vanda suavis*, given to him by the wife of a man he had cleared on a murder rap." That candy-scented vanda, originally from southeast Asia, had charms that infected its new owner. With a purple lip and petals with brushstroke spots of magenta, Nero Wolfe could *feel* the color, suggesting that among his many genius qualities, perhaps he had a form of synesthesia.

The vanda survived only briefly in the growing conditions of Wolfe's office. When it died, it threw down the horticultural gauntlet. Wolfe took up the challenge. He bought twenty more plants and added the first small greenhouse on the roof. From that point, Wolfe's appetite for orchids was never sated.

Collecting rare specimens of the varied tribes of Orchidaceae requires deep pockets and drives Wolfe's insistence on large fees for his investigative services. He is relentless in his pursuit of unusual varieties, acquiring them from commercial nurseries or cutting out the middleman and buying them directly from plant explorers. Once he agreed to take on a case in exchange for a set of three rare black orchids. He sometimes barters plants with other private hybridizers. While he is known for occasional orchid largesse, bestowing blossoms for sentimental or practical reasons, his plants are not for sale.

Many real people of the society pages, including Doris Duke and several members of the du Pont family, shared Wolfe's fictional compulsion. Through the early decades of the twentieth century, orchids became a symbol, if not *the* symbol, of luxury in America and beyond. They were unusual and expensive, with exquisite, often scented blooms, redolent of jungle and tropics. At the time—well before mass production tissue culture brought them to supermarkets and big box stores—they had mystique. They were favorites of Madison Avenue, used to market whiskey, California citrus fruits, leather goods, couture, cosmetics, and perfume. In 1937, Green Giant advertised its canned peas as "The Orchid of the Pea Family." When Rex Stout chose orchid growing as his detective's passion, he picked a plant that had already captured the American imagination.

The Nero Wolfe stories teem with orchids. Michael Bishop, a member of the devoted fan base known collectively as "The Wolfe Pack," cataloged every instance and type of orchid, organized by title in Rex Stout's Nero Wolfe oeuvre. Topping the list are the fifteen orchid varieties in the first Wolfe novel, *Fer-de-Lance* and the twenty-two in *Murder by the Book*. As to species, those in the genus *Phalaenopsis* get the most frequent nod, in particular the cultivar 'Aphrodite' with its long-blooming racemes of white flowers.

Wolfe also hybridizes orchids, breeding and propagating them in sterile conditions that seem closer to laboratory than plant nursery. Discipline and patience are among the demands of his "concubines," as he occasionally refers to them. His orchid crosses are also a cross to bear; it can take up to seven years for one of his hybrid-produced seedlings to mature and, at last, to bloom.

Unlike Sherlock Holmes and his occasional violin practice, Wolfe devotes part of each day to his orchids in the plant rooms. He spends four hours precisely, divided into two sessions: from 9:00 to 11:00 in the morning and 4:00 to 6:00 post meridiem. Those who hope to see him book an appointment through Archie for a time that does not conflict with the orchids—or meals—as Wolfe rarely alters his schedule.

Wolfe is also a gastronome, and, as such, herbs appear on menus in many of his stories. Lunch might offer a meat entrée with béchamel sauce and chervil. The squash side dish at dinner might be garnished with dill. However, Wolfe does not deign to squander greenhouse bench space with edibles; his plant rooms are reserved for orchids. If resident-chef Fritz Brenner runs out of fresh herbs in the kitchen, Archie sets out to find them in a shop, rather than fetch them from the greenhouse on the top floor.

Rex Stout published his last Nero Wolfe novel in 1975. Twenty years later, a new gardening detective emerged in the Texas Hill Country with Susan Wittig Albert's *Thyme of Death*, released in 1992. The horticultural mystery genre was, by this time, well established. Albert's lead character, like Wolfe, enjoys cooking and eating with herbs and, like Cadfael, appreciates their useful and medicinal properties. But unlike Miss Marple, amateur sleuth and horticulturist, China Bayles is a professional—a former attorney who has embarked on a second career.

CHINA BAYLES

*When people ask me, "Why herbs?" I give them the short answer:
"Because plants don't talk back." When they ask, "Why Pecan Springs?"
I reply, "Because it seemed so crime-free and peaceful."*

—CHINA BAYLES IN *QUEEN ANNE'S LACE* (2018)

At the opening of Susan Wittig Albert's savvy, long-running series, her protagonist China Bayles has walked away from her high-pressure job as a big-city criminal defense attorney and remade herself. Two years earlier, she had relocated from Houston to the rural county seat of Pecan Springs and acquired a historic building on Crockett Street. She is now the proud proprietor of Thyme and Seasons, a business selling herbs for all reasons: fresh, dried, potted, and potions. It may not line her pockets, but it does nourish her soul.

Pecan Springs, however, is far from peaceful. Like St. Mary Mead and so many other small towns of detective fiction, the place is downright crime ridden. The number of murders makes one ponder the impact on the population count. A made-up place, Pecan Springs is the seat of fictional Adams County, somewhere between Austin and San Antonio. It is a sort of Everytown, USA. Pecan Springs has a courthouse square, a busy commercial center, and is a college town. And it is here that China Bayles has embarked on her plant pilgrimage.

The name "Pecan Springs" fits the bill, in terms of actual native flora and geology of the hill country. The pecan, *Carya illinoinensis*, reigns as the state tree of Texas as well as the town's namesake. Natural springs and lakes abound courtesy of the limestone strata of the subterranean Edwards Aquifer. Along the eroded eastern side of the Edwards Plateau, the hill country undulates through a large area deep in the heart of the Lone Star State. Albert finds many opportunities to interject satisfying mini lessons on the region's plant life and topography.

As Thyme and Seasons expands, China transforms the property around her building. It was good-bye lawn; hello, herb garden! To be more precise, *gardens*. There is a garden for tea, a garden for the butterflies, another for chefs, and still another for textile artists interested in natural dyes. You can probably picture it. Think of an herb garden design, and you will likely conjure a geometric grid—a square or rectangle is the most common— subdivided into practical, manageable beds, something akin to a traditional quilt pattern. Brother Cadfael would have approved.

This type of garden had a rebirth in popularity around the turn of the twentieth century. In England, it reemerged as part of the Arts and Crafts movement; in America, it was a fixture of the Colonial Revival. We learn in the first book of the series, *Thyme of Death* (1992), that like so many gardeners, China's love of gardening came from her grandmother. Nostalgia is a powerful motivator.

Grandmother—whether Bayles or on the distaff side—would have been a fictional contemporary of nonfiction garden writer Alice Morse Earle, whose *Old Time Gardens* (1901) celebrated tidy, boxwood-edged beds and the traditional flowers and herbs of America's colonial past. A white picket fence was de rigueur; a sundial atop a white column was an appropriate focal point. The plants in China's herb beds attract both pollinators and people to her shop, bolstering sales along the way.

China Bayles finds other ways to build her clientele. She writes a newsletter and pens a gardening column for the local newspaper, the *Enterprise*. If you live in town and run a community group, say the Friends of the Pecan Springs Public Library, you can book one of her herb-inspired lectures. Selected herb lore that protagonist China—read Susan Wittig Albert herself—collects provides the chapter headings of the novels. *Rosemary Remembered*, for example, incorporates quotes from Shakespeare, Sir Thomas More, poet Robert Herrick, and assorted modern and antique herbals. As useful plants, herbs have held a place in botanical literature as far back as humans have put quill to parchment or reed to papyrus.

In the Americas, cultivating herbs has had a long history, and Susan Wittig Albert weaves it into her plots. Tribal peoples grew them. When European colonists arrived and spread from sea to shining sea, they brought an influx of their own herbal species, carrying the seeds and cuttings that would offer flavorings for the pantry and remedies for the medicine chest. Some of the plants, like Queen Anne's lace, naturalized so effectively that the average person would identify it as an all-American wildflower. (It was

from Albert and her inimitable China Bayles that I learned that this carrot-family relative was widely used in pre-pharmaceutical family planning.)

As with *Queen Anne's Lace* (the book), each China Bayles novel spotlights one plant species. If you pick up *Rueful Death*, you can be assured that the rue herb will be woven artfully through the plot, and that you will learn a great deal about how to grow and use it as the action unfolds. Some of the books include recipes, as Bayles makes them, for their titular herbs.

While the energetic China discovers that her laid-back country lifestyle has given her more time to enjoy cooking and life in general, her under-standing of the criminal justice system and her analytical skills do not go dormant. Yes, murders keep cropping up in Pecan Springs, and Bayles is a natural-born sleuth. She can't resist investigating any mystery that comes her way, aided by her encyclopedic knowledge of herbs and the help of her friends. Pecan Springs has provided such fertile ground that several of the minor characters featured in the China Bayles books now star in series of their own, including Ruby Wilcox, owner of the New Age shop, Crystal Cave, and Jessica Nelson, *Pecan Springs Enterprise* crime reporter. All from the prolific pen of Susan Wittig Albert.

There are more detectives, both amateurs and pros, that are or have been devoted to plants. Perhaps it is because plant people—I put myself in this category—lean toward the obsessive, a definite plus for investigators. Martin Walker invented Chief Inspector Bruno Courrèges who tends his potager in the Périgord. Alan Bradley provided his eleven-year-old sleuth—well, almost eleven—with a gardening sidekick named Arthur Wesley Dogger. In the course of *Lucy Clark Will Not Apologize,* author Margo Rabb has her young detective learn how to garden. One of Charlotte MacLeod's detectives is a professor of agronomy—crop and soil science—at a New England agricultural college. Two horticulturists, Rosemary Boxer and Laura Thyme, solve garden crimes over three seasons and twenty-two episodes of ITV's *Rosemary & Thyme.* There are horticultural detectives who have operated in the past and present, at home and abroad. They tend to occupy the cozier class of mystery, as opposed to noir or hard-boiled. But whatever the category, they often find themselves in gardens. Whether elaborate or simple, famous or obscure, there is no better crime scene for a horticulturally minded sleuth to investigate than a garden.

SETTING

Garden Scenes of the Crime

A garden has been a stand-in for paradise as far back as the sixth century BC when Cyrus the Great built his palace gardens at Pasargadae, the royal center of the first Persian empire. Three hundred years later, Alexander the Great conquered the place. He was so impressed that he had his historian, Herodotus, capture descriptions of its gardens for posterity. The word "paradise" winds its linguistic way back through Greek and Latin to its origins in Cyrus's ancient Persia, when the word connoted an enclosed space, girded with walls. With the addition of water and beautiful plants, the meaning has expanded over time into heaven on earth.

Now take that Edenic setting and overlay a feeling of unease. Dread. Or add something nasty, something, let's say, like a dead body. Contrast magnifies the horror. Writers have long employed this "paradise lost" contradiction where a garden shifts from inviting to ominous. In the Book of Genesis, Cain, a tiller of the ground, slew his brother Abel in the field.

William Shakespeare got into the act. He chose bucolic murder settings twice in Hamlet. Old king Hamlet shuffles off the mortal coil in his orchard. Poisoned. His son Hamlet then performs an on-stage garden murder, a play-within-a-play, to catch the conscience of the villain. Author John Berendt took a similar line, choosing *Midnight in the Garden of Good and Evil* as the title for his Savannah, Georgia, true crime saga. Writers of detective fictions have planted bodies in their plots ranging from the humblest community garden beds to the most famous display gardens in the world.

A SUNKEN GARDEN

If a garden crime scene was good enough for the Bible and the Bard, it was good enough for Agatha Christie. A devotee of Shakespeare, her mysteries often allude to his works. She used a garden backdrop in *Hallowe'en Party* (1969) for Hercule Poirot, another of her star detectives. Poirot's description reads like a scary version of *A Midsummer Night's Dream*:

> Somehow, he thought, this was not an English garden in which he was sitting... Here, if you were staging a scene in the theatre, you would have your nymphs, your fauns, you would have Greek beauty, you would have fear too.

Compared to Miss Marple, Poirot was Christie's anti-gardener. The word "fussy" comes to mind. It is hard to picture the Monsieur grubbing out weeds or picking off cabbage worms. The only instance of him engaged in active horticulture is a memorable scene in *The Murder of Roger Ackroyd* (1926); standing in his potager, the then-retired detective hurls his frustrating vegetable marrows over the neighbor's fence. *Mon Dieu*! In *Hallowe'en*

Party, published over forty years later, he is back in character, observing gardens but never touching a plant.

He was Christie's most productive protagonist, appearing in eighty-seven works spanning five decades. Hercule Poirot is the only detective of fiction whose death was honored by a front-page obituary in the *New York Times*. He is precise in habit and dapper in dress or, as he says, *soigné*. His attire indicates a character best suited to an urban, urbane existence. Does the mustachioed Belgian bring sturdy outdoor shoes for tramping the lanes when his friend, mystery writer Ariadne Oliver, calls him to the country in *Hallowe'en Party*? No, he packs his pair of stylish patent leathers.

Oliver had arranged the rendezvous after a children's Halloween party ended in murder. Someone had drowned a thirteen-year-old girl, a girl who boasted of once seeing a murder. Poirot follows that thread. Reviewing past cases with the local constabulary, he focuses on a long-unsolved killing of a twenty-eight-year-old law clerk. The body had been discovered in an unused well in a defunct quarry, since transformed into a sunken garden.

New gardens often contain vestigial remains of their predecessors, clues to previous gardeners and occupants of the property. In my garden, for example, a grove of dark Norway spruce tower over the front of the house. It is not a tree I would have chosen. Not native to northern New Jersey, it is messy in every season with a spring deluge of pollen and steady deposits of needles and cones for the rest of the year. Yet the trees remain, silent reminders of past owners and their horticultural devices and desires. Over time I have carved out a spring shade border among their roots in the dry, acidic soil.

In *Hallowe'en Party*, the designer, on behalf of his client, has taken a quarry with geologic and industrial history and overlaid an enchanting, designed landscape, rich with paths and plants. The well with its murderous past is hidden, but still present.

Christie hints at the inspiration for the "sunk garden," as she calls it. The owner of the property, we are told, had seen a garden on a National Trust garden tour. The quarry in its new guise reminds Poirot of a garden on the southwest coast of Ireland in Bantry Bay. While not mentioned by name, Agatha Christie—through her character—is describing Ilnacullin, an island garden about a kilometer offshore, sheltered in Glengarriff Harbour. There, classicist designer Harold Peto created a sunken Italian garden for owners Annan and Violet Bryce in grand Edwardian fashion.

Agatha Christie visited Ilnacullin in 1959, later transforming her impressions into the scene of a crime for Poirot's investigative skills. He notes that the sunken garden of the novel is expertly planned and planted, a quiet elegance seemingly natural but in fact contrived. Like Ilnacullin, it harkens back to a classical age with a planting palette of modern rarities: *Parrotia* for the autumn, Asian maples with red and golden foliage. An unlikely spot for murder. Poirot can be arrogant, but he is rarely wrong. The sunken garden with its magic, almost pagan atmosphere keeps drawing him back.

A GERTRUDE JEKYLL GARDEN

Designs by other famous gardeners take their place in the mystery canon. Take the real-life artist-turned-garden-stylist Gertrude Jekyll (1843–1932), for example, who established herself as the doyenne of the English perennial border. ("Jekyll" rhymes with "treacle," even though Robert Louis

Stevenson, a friend of her brother Walter, borrowed the name for his *Strange Case of Dr. Jekyll and Mr. Hyde*, which is typically pronounced as rhyming with "freckle.") In *The Mantrap Garden*, published in 1986, author John Sherwood attributed a fictional garden design to Jekyll. He called it "Monk's Mead," and wrote of a murder that had taken place there. Enter Sherwood's sleuth: the plant expert Celia Grant, who has just agreed to be a trustee for the garden.

The story opens in the unspecified present. In the same family for two generations, Monk's Mead is now operated as a charity open to the public. Maintaining a Jekyll garden—or any historic garden—is a Sisyphean labor of love and money. It can be a burden, a trap for the owners. By the time Celia Grant is invited to be a trustee, the borders are disintegrating. Bindweed strangles flower stems. A vandal has been spraying weed killer on some of the original shrubs. Someone has been filling gaps in the Long Border with red and white pelargoniums. Miss Jekyll would be turning over in her grave.

Sherwood sprinkles facts about Gertrude Jekyll's design aesthetic and plant preferences throughout the book. "The Garland," her favorite rose, grows at Monk's Mead. Its gardens include many of her signature plant combinations. Take, for example, the *Yucca gloriosa* and *Euphorbia wulfenii* paired with red hot pokers. Jekyll's planting plans glowed with subtle coloration; they were also opportunities to market plants from the nursery she ran at her Surrey home, Munstead Wood, shod in her well-worn gardening boots.

Jekyll understood the subtleties of plants. While she might have been bemused at her own appearance in crime fiction, she understood the "mysterious beauty of colouring" of blue plants like juniper. Blue was for depth, for an undertone of secrecy. She also knew that her clients could ruin a planting plan. For color-themed rooms such as those at the fictional Monk's Mead, she preached:

> People will sometimes spoil some garden project for the sake of a word. For instance a Blue Garden may be hungering for a group of white lilies, or for something of palest lemon yellow, but is not allowed to have it because it is called the Blue Garden and there must be no flowers in it but blue flowers. Surely the business of the Blue Garden is to be beautiful as well as blue.

So prevalent is Jekyll's work throughout the novel that John Sherwood includes this passage—an excerpt from her *Colour in the Flower Garden*—and a number of others in *The Mantrap Garden*. It makes one wonder if Jekyll would have considered murdering a client.

While the motives are dated and the plot contorted, much of the action takes place in the garden at Monk's Mead, and the setting makes the book worthy of a read. Celia's horticultural expertise comes into play during her investigations. She finds the famous Munstead primroses, bred by Miss Jekyll, weed-infested and in need of dividing. A Jekyll-planted magnolia specimen is brutally hacked. The owner, oddly, is directing suspicion away from his gardeners. And then the body of a French tourist is found in the garden with a kitchen knife in his back.

The Wild Garden at Monk's Mead is the scene of a climax worthy of Daphne du Maurier or Charlotte Brontë. In its aftermath, the garden's owners are relieved of their historic garden and look forward to unburdened lives with a small garden crammed full of the garish, multi-colored bedding plants Miss Jekyll detested.

A BED OF BLUE FLOWERS

In *Password to Larkspur Lane* (1933) by Carolyn Keene, lead character Nancy Drew has entered a flower show. After the judging, Nancy sees:

> Attached to her bouquet of larkspur was a dark-blue satin ribbon with the inscription FIRST PRIZE!
>
> "Nancy, that's wonderful," her father said. "Congratulations! Maybe you ought to give up solving mysteries and raise flowers."
>
> "Not a chance," she said.

I was nine years old when publisher Gross and Dunlap re-released *Password to Larkspur Lane*, one of the nearly two hundred Nancy Drew mysteries in the franchise. The heroine has been a spunky, independent role model for several generations of young heroines-in-training. *Password to Larkspur Lane* is the tenth book in the series, first released in 1933 but revised and reissued in the edition that I remember.

Its author is its own mystery. That's because Carolyn Keene is the authorial equivalent of Betty Crocker. She never existed. It is a made-up name coined by the real father of the series, publisher Edward Stratemeyer. A marketing whiz, Stratemeyer invented many famous young adult series including *Nancy Drew* and *The Hardy Boys*. He hired ghostwriters to complete them.

Stratemeyer sketched out the first Nancy Drew, *The Secret of the Old Clock*, in the 1920s and hired Mildred Wirt, a University of Iowa–trained journalist, to complete the manuscript. She and all the Stratemeyer syndicate's freelancers were contractually sworn to secrecy, an agreement that held until a lawsuit in 1979. (Since then, writers like Susan Wittig Albert who take a turn as Carolyn Keene are free to share their part in the series.)

The publisher's daughter, Harriet Stratemeyer Adams, was a Wellesley College alumna with a BA in English composition, which she put to good use in the family business. Adams assumed editorial control of the *Nancy Drew* series after her father's death in 1930, overseeing the next sixty books. She insisted that they be educational as well as entertaining. One reviewer described Nancy Drew as a renaissance teen; she seemed to excel at everything. The subject of *Password to Larkspur Lane* is flower gardening.

The most horticulturally intensive of the series, the story opens with our eighteen-year-old detective selecting the best of her larkspur to enter in the flower show. Its electric blue spires shimmer in her flower bed. She muses that she might have been picking larkspur in ancient Greece at the Temple of Apollo at Delphi, conferring another name, *Delphinium*, to the species.

An injured homing pigeon falls near Nancy's garden. A message around its banded leg reads, "Blue bells will be singing horses." Very strange. As her father observes, Nancy attracts mysteries like nectar attracts pollinators.

While she would always prefer solving a mystery to gardening, in this book Nancy has flowers on the brain. Her neighbor reminds her that bluebells are like larkspurs and hollyhocks, old-fashioned flowers, long popular in American gardens especially since the Colonial Revival movement that began around the United States centennial celebrations in 1876.

If you are wondering about the horticultural zone of Nancy Drew's larkspur, she lives in the undefined American Midwest, in a town called River Heights. Some fans have insisted that it is in Illinois; others argue for Ohio. Wherever it is, Nancy likely lives in zone 5 or 6.

In *Password to Larkspur Lane*, bluebells and larkspur serve twin functions as plants and keys to a mystery. They are the clues that Nancy and her intrepid chums chase to an old estate with blue flowers bordering a white colonial residence on a road named Larkspur Lane. It is a beautiful property with groves of trees, floral beds, and lawns—beautiful except for the sinister electric fence that surrounds it and the wealthy senior patients who are imprisoned there. While cliffhangers abound, everything turns out in the end, which, after all, is one of the reasons that the mystery format is so appealing. Unlike in a garden, where sometimes the weeds win or the prized specimen succumbs, in the world of the murder mystery, justice is served.

THE WHITE GARDEN
AT SISSINGHURST CASTLE

A garden of a different color is front and center in Stephanie Barron's *The White Garden*. The garden of the novel's title—the White Garden at Sissinghurst Castle—is the stuff of legend, and arguably England's most famous garden room. Its creators, Vita Sackville-West and Harold Nicolson, are equally legendary, both for their committed, unconventional marriage and for the garden that they created between the 1930s and the 1960s.

What gardener is perfectly satisfied with their garden? Famous or not, Sackville-West wasn't satisfied with hers. In 1954, when both *Gardening Illustrated* and *Country Life* wanted to showcase Sissinghurst, Vita wrote a letter to Harold, musing:

> It *is* funny, isn't it, that our own dear garden should be taking its place among the better known gardens of England? Oh, if only we could have the last twenty years all over again! We wouldn't make any change in the design, but I should like to go back and make a great many changes in the planting. Beastly garden.

As the basis for her plot, Stephanie Barron connects the creation of the White Garden to Vita's intimate friend, fellow gardener, and sometime lover, Virginia Woolf.

The White Garden is a literary mystery of gardens. It explores the entanglements of the Bloomsbury Circle, a group of artists and writers including Vita and Virginia, often described as "living in squares and loving in triangles." It delves into Woolf's final days in 1941. Her suicide, walking into the River Ouse, pockets filled with stones, is well known. Barron recounts an alternate history through her protagonist, Jo Bellamy, a present-day American garden designer.

Bellamy arrives at Sissinghurst to study its planting plans for a Long Island client. In searching through boxes of papers in a Sissinghurst outbuilding, Bellamy comes across an old diary that seems to be in Virginia Woolf's handwriting. But the final entry is a day after Woolf's supposed suicide! When Bellamy pockets the diary, the gears of the plot begin to turn.

The reader encounters Sissinghurst's White Garden late in the season as Jo Bellamy explores it. A garden in autumn has a mournful cast. The growing season ebbs away, like the end of a party with guests straggling out. Dregs of summer with a few late arrivals, but the main event is over. Overnight, white flowers blacken from frost. Color leaches from stem and leaf, leaving pallid, skeletal remains and touches of red. From her sixteenth-century tower-turned-writing-studio overlooking the garden, Sackville-West once wrote:

> Autumn in felted slipper shuffles on,
> Muted yet fiery—Autumn's character.
> Brown as a monk yet flaring as a whore,
> And in the distance blue as Raphael's robe
> Tender around the Virgin.

Jo Bellamy describes autumn as bittersweet. Some glory in the late season garden—as contemporary Dutch designer Piet Oudolf celebrates herbaceous perennials in their gray garb—but it can't help but summon specters of age and its inevitable successor.

Autumn reveals the bones of Sissinghurst in the book. Crossing the garden's threshold, Bellamy has a sense of transition, of passing to the underworld through a kind of Gothic tunnel. She strolls its Yew Rondel, a round room of tall yew hedges pierced by four openings, and along Harold's famed Lime Walk. (Lime is the British common name for linden, the genus *Tilia*.) Two mythological statues, the Bacchante and the Vestal Virgin, are focal points in the gardens and in the mystery. Among the clipped boxwoods we stop with Bellamy to admire the many roses, peonies, and lilies that were Vita's favorites.

The suicide of Bellamy's grandfather hangs over her work. Her grandfather was a lifelong gardener and her mentor, and he had worked at Sissinghurst as a young man. Following scraps and traces that include Wolff's diary, Jo finds clues hinting at connections between two deaths, past and present.

With a rich cast of supporting characters—an Oxford don, an American billionaire, two Sotheby's antiquarian book experts, and Sissinghurst's head gardener—a literary chase ensues. There are flashbacks to Vita and Harold, Virginia and her husband Leonard. As Jo Bellamy untangles the story of her grandfather's youth, the original, if fictional, inspiration for the White Garden is revealed.

Virginia Woolf's death haunts another horticultural mystery, *The Lost Garden* by Helen Humphreys. The novel is set in 1941, just after Wolff's suicide. Rather than using a renowned location like Sissinghurst, Humphreys, a Canadian poet, chose to fashion a garden of her own.

A GARDEN OF LOVE AND LOSS

The thing about gardens is that everyone thinks that they
go on growing, that in winter they sleep and in spring they rise.
But it's more that they die and return. They lose themselves.
They haunt themselves.

—*THE LOST GARDEN* BY HELEN HUMPHREYS

The bones of neglected gardens beckon. It may be a throwback to childhood ambitions—"I want to be a paleontologist" or "I want to be an archeologist"—for digs and discoveries, for shards of times past. A forgotten column base conjures a pergola, a curved section of balustrade hints at cocktails and evening dress. Wisteria, scrambling through an empty lot, seems to pose questions. Who planted it, tended it, first inhaled its heady aroma?

Gardens are layered art in a living medium. They change with the tick of a clock and the turn of a calendar page. Irises lift their elegant standards one morning and shrivel by the next. A border, spare in spring, burgeons in the honey-heat of summer. Over sweeps of years, trees stretch out their canopies to shade out neighbors, or die to open a swath of light. In *The Lost Garden*, author Helen Humphreys ponders the layers of a fictional English estate garden as one part of its landscape disappears, and another reemerges.

Her main character is Gwen Davis, a graduate of a horticultural college in the employ of London's Royal Horticultural Society. In 1941, Davis exchanges her botanical research—potential cures for parsnip blight—for a position in the Women's Land Army. Gwen is posted as a supervisor to a Devon estate called Mosel.

The Women's Land Army is historical fact. The War Office created it during the First World War and revived it during the Second to address the agricultural—and to a lesser extent, horticultural—labor shortage. *The Journal of the Kew Guild*, a publication of the Royal Botanic Gardens, Kew, published a spoof of Rudyard Kipling's famous garden verse in 1941:

> Now Adam was a gardener, and God who made him sees
> That half a gardener's proper work is done upon his knees;
> But with Adam gone to fight the foe and only home on leave
> The proper one to kneel and plant and grow our food is—EVE!

Gwen disembarks the train at the local station, lugging the volumes of her library with her from London. As someone more comfortable with books than people, she couldn't leave her old friends behind. Virginia Woolf's *To the Lighthouse* was among them—Woolf's suicide two months before the novel's action gets substantial comment—as was Ellen Willmott's weighty, illustrated two-volume tome, *The Genus Rosa*. Ellen Willmott (1858–1934), another of the matron saints of British horticulture, is now largely forgotten.

Born into wealth, Wilmott devoted her life and substantial inheritance to horticulture. She made three extensive gardens at three residences, was a force in the Royal Horticultural Society, and funded several plant-collecting expeditions. In 1904, when the Linnean Society at last opened its door to women, she was one of the first to step through. But her ending wasn't rosy. Ellen Willmott's addiction—it is said that she grew more than 100,000 different plants—overran her life. By the end she was bankrupt, eccentric, and reclusive, though still gardening. In *The Lost Garden*, Helen Humphreys links her main character, Gwen Davis, to Woolf and Willmott, two extraordinary, complicated women.

Each night, Davis shares her bed with Willmott's *The Genus Rosa*, finding comfort in its heft, its solidity. She is an experienced gardener but a management neophyte. With the women on her team, she is awkward, if not bumbling. To keep them straight, she silently confers names of appropriate potato varieties on each one. A large, competent woman becomes Lumper; an enthusiastic blonde is Golden Wonder. For her dark hair and kitchen skills, another is dubbed Victualette Noir.

The potato metaphor is apt. Britain's "Dig for Victory" campaign is underway. Gwen's principal responsibility is to get the estate's landscaped acreage plowed and planted with seed potatoes. As the action unfolds, Mosel's rolling lawns are converted to potato production.

Not all garden spaces go to spuds. There are remnant ornamental plantings at Mosel, though much diminished from their original. Captain Raley, a Canadian officer billeted in the requisitioned manor house, finds turn-of-the-century landscape plans for the estate. Gwen finds an old ledger, with twenty-five gardeners listed on staff in 1914. By the end of the Great War all but six names had been crossed out, killed in the campaigns. After two decades and amid the new war, the maze and water garden are gone; the wild garden is indistinguishable from woodland. One can barely distinguish the garden rooms—kitchen, cutting, orchard—and the yew walk that separates them from the park.

A drift of anemones leads Davis to the lost garden of the novel's title, tucked between the orchard and the brooding darkness of the yews. This hidden garden is overrun with nettles, though some of the original plants and built features persist. Only hints remain of the designer's work. Gwen becomes obsessed with the hidden space. It is a garden in a code that she works to decipher. Having no Rosetta Stone, she must rely on its plants.

The original plantings of the lost garden emerge from the weeds, silent and expressive. Their flowers speak with scent: sweetbrier and lavender, saffron crocus, the plum-perfumed *Iris graminea*, a damask 'Madame Hardy' with fragrant old-rose aroma. They remind Gwen of a line from Virgil: "Let there be Gardens to tempt them, breathing saffron flowers." Floral nectar has a language of its own, hard-wired to our senses in a wordless vocabulary. Our sense of smell triggers emotional memories, olfactory explosions in the brain.

Gwen might have chosen another quote from the same book of the Georgics, "These ardent passions and these prodigious contests/A little handful of dust will lay to rest." The dead laid to rest in the handful of dust that is *The Lost Garden* are memories, not bodies. It is a commemorative space. The beloved was a casualty of the first war, unnamed and now unknown. More recent grief is Raley's, who lost his lover earlier

in this war and, with Gwen's help, plants a magnolia for him at Mosel. Through the course of the novel, Gwen finds her own longing, love, loss. But like the garden, she survives.

AN ITALIAN VILLA GARDEN

Gardens often act as stages. They serve as backdrops for fêtes, trysts, and performances. In the gardens of the Palace of Versailles, Louis XIV once held a six-day party that featured, among other spectacles, the premieres of Molière's opera *Tartuffe* and a ballet by Lully. The patrons and creators of Italian Renaissance gardens also built dramatic backstories into their designs. One such garden is the Florentine villa garden that serves as the setting for Mark Mills's *The Savage Garden* (2007).

These villa gardens are typically fashioned on allegories drawn from Greek and Roman mythology; their meanings implicit rather than explicit. Designers of this style relied on statue, inscription, suggestion, and symbol to convey their messages.

In *The Savage Garden*, an allegorical garden serves as both the crime scene and the source of the solution. Author Mark Mills moves his protagonist, the bright but lazy Adam Strickland, from the University of Cambridge to a villa garden in the Tuscan hills. It is 1958, and memories of the Second World War are very much alive. Professor Crispin Leonard, Adam's art history tutor, suggests a garden at the Villa Docci as thesis topic. The professor had spent a summer there as a student, sixty years earlier. The garden had been laid out in the sixteenth century by a husband to the memory of Flora, his dead wife.

For background reading, Professor Leonard directs Adam to Ovid's *Metamorphoses* and Dante's *Divine Comedy*. Adam reads the latter in a translation by Dorothy L(eigh) Sayers, a scholar of literature who was among the first female graduates of Oxford. Sayers is better known for her detective fiction, of course. But more about her later.

When Adam arrives, the villa does not disappoint. It is elegant. The widow of a descendant, the sophisticated Signora Docci, is there to receive him. One of the Signora's sons had been killed at the villa near the end of the war during the German retreat; two other children and a granddaughter still live nearby. Around these characters and those from four centuries earlier, the plot unfolds.

But what of the gardens at Villa Docci? There are cypresses, those characteristic verticals in much of the Italian landscape. The entrance to the villa is an avenue of cypresses; it narrows as it approaches the house, tricking the eye with a forced perspective. Tall, tight hedges of yew provide green architecture, forming outdoor rooms around the residence and its earlier terraced gardens. A marble pool reflects its surroundings.

The garden at the center of the book is a *memento mori*, a reminder that all earthly things come to an end, at least in their current state. It is built into a hillside, crowned with an amphitheater and a triumphal arch. The subject of the garden is depicted by a statue of Flora on a plinth. The sculpture represents Federico Docci's departed wife as the mythological mistress of flowers, transformed by the west wind, Zephyrus, after he rapes and weds her. More figures of gods and demi-gods inhabit the garden and direct the eye:

> Having laid out this new kingdom, Federico had then dedicated it to Flora, goddess of flowers, and populated it with the characters from ancient mythology over whom she held sway: Hyacinth, Narcissus, and Adonis. All had died tragically, and all lived on in the flowers that burst from the earth where their blood had spilled—the same flowers that still enameled the ground in their respective areas of the garden every springtime. Their stories cast a melancholy pall over the garden.

The tale they tell is disorienting. Apollo, the sun god, mourns the murdered youth Hyacinth. The enraptured Narcissus stares into a pool close by the temple of the nymph Echo. He fades into the flower that bears his name, she into the reverberation that calls out to him, unanswered. Venus, goddess of love, holds the beautiful, expiring Adonis. Apollo, frequently busy with his amours, pursues Daphne as she morphs into a laurel tree, saved by her river god father. For stories of love, vengeance and violence, modern mystery writers have nothing on the ancients.

Paths direct the visitor's progress downhill in the villa garden. The plants are dark, almost black: ilex, laurel, and other evergreens. Dense groves, offset by open glens, propel the visitor from dark to light. Are these entrances to the underworld or sacred groves, hell or heaven, requiem or gloria? Distant past, recent past, present. There are secrets and lies, betrayals and murders buried in the villa and its village. As the sometimes-narcissistic Adam delves into the art history of the place, he finds more than one Italian mystery to unravel. He also finds love.

If you visit Italy, you will not find a villa named Docci. It is a brainchild of the author. In *The Savage Garden*, Mark Mills alludes to a similar garden

not far from Rome: the Villa Bomarzo with its enigmatic *sacro bosco*. Vincino Farnese began the construction after the death of his wife, Giulia, in the 1550s. Its woodland is populated with gods and monsters, including the infamous "Mouth of Hell," a cave-sized sculpture with both an injunction from Dante to the damned and picnic seating inside the mammoth hellmouth. Bomarzo is on my must-see garden list, should I get back to Italy one of these days.

A GARDEN GROWS IN BROOKLYN

A recent stellar addition to garden settings in detective fiction is James McBride's *Deacon King Kong*. It is peppered with murderous intent, though there isn't a murder per se. Laced with good guys, bad guys, and wise guys, it combines mystery and comedy. The leading man is Cuffy Lambkin, a man of many nicknames: Deacon King Kong for his position with Five Ends Baptist Church and preference for the strong local hooch, old Sportcoat for age and attire, Plant Man for prowess with all things green. The novel's garden settings are spaced throughout, in the fictional Causeway Housing Project and its adjoining South Brooklyn neighborhood in New York City.

A shooting takes place in the plaza between the project's towers. The specifics of the crime are laid out in the opening paragraph: the victim, a local drug dealer; the weapon, an ancient .38 caliber Colt revolver; the shooter, Cuffy himself. Why? Why would this flawed but loveable deacon shoot Deems Clemens, who, as drug dealers go, was relatively benign, not to mention being a local kid?

Several other mysteries bloom as the answers unfold, mysteries surrounded by gardens. An Italian widow, mother to a local mobster, collects

wild plants. She cultivates them around
her nearby home. Some days Cuffy is her
garden helper, with tasks like digging the
abundant pokeweed for her home-brewed
cure-alls.

Nights, an evocative southern garden
disturbs Cuffy's sleep, a symbol tied to his
dead wife Hettie. The dream-garden is filled
with plants that had permeated their court-
ship. Her spirit conjures up scents heavy in the South Carolina air of their
youth. Spicebush, sweetgum, cucumber tree. He could identify any plant
by its smell, day or night. Her favorite had always been a nocturnal flower,
white, round, and suffused with fragrance.

Cuffy's friend Rufus remembers Hettie arriving at the Causeway, so
many years ago. She was herself a transplant, and she had a vision of a garden, a garden that her Cuffy was going to make for her. Rufus says:

> That's when Hettie made that big yard out behind the church that's all
> weeds now. She wanted a big garden back there. She said you was gonna
> come up and fill it with all sorts of collards and yams and even some
> special kind of flower, something you can see in the dark, I forget what
> it's called now.

Cuffy remembers—moonflower.

The supporting cast is rich: Hot Sausage, the Causeway's janitor; Sister
Gee, pillar of the Five Ends Baptist Church; Soup Lopez, the gentle giant
just released from prison; Potts, the honest Irish cop, ready for retirement;
Tommy "the Elephant" Elephante, an old-fashioned Italian mobster with
a heart of gold, and his herbalist mother. There is a lost treasure, specifica-
tions unknown, hidden somewhere in the neighborhood by the Elephant's

father Guido. And don't forget the question: why *did* Cuffy Lambkin shoot Deems Clemens? This is a book about romance and respect, religion and race, the meaning of community, home, and garden. There are promises broken and, in the end, promises kept. One of those promises is a garden that finally, belatedly, gets planted.

◆ ◆ ◆

Sometimes a mystery that seems to have a garden setting turns out to be a blind alley. It is like catching a glimpse of a garden that isn't open to visitors. In *The Yellow Room Conspiracy*, British mystery writer Peter Dickinson opens his story on a summer day in the garden. Paul Ackerley, a retired businessman, stands in this middle of his Yellow Border (capitalized in the book). He is trying to banish bindweed on a summer day. If you have ever been plagued with bindweed, you'll know it is a nemesis. This weedy relation of the morning glory grows like a curse, winding itself amongst desirable plants in an upward climb for dominance. Paul, speaking in the first person, is ready to employ chemical warfare:

> So I was poised in the midst of all the late July uprush (I keep my borders pretty crammed) with my feet twisted into two small clear patches, and my hands, having disentwined the growing tips of the bindweed and eased them into the bag and sprayed them there, now trying to withdraw them and at the same time shake any excess poison from them back into the bag so that it didn't drip elsewhere.

This description, in the first paragraph of the first chapter, foreshadows the rest of the part-espionage and part-crime novel.

Only a few other hints about the garden emerge, sad to say. The steel-blue heads of his eryngium set off the daisy-like petals of the orange and mahogany

The Gazebo, published in 1958.

rudbeckia. The chalky soil has eliminated the need to cope with rhododendrons and azaleas. Dickinson name-drops landscape gardener Humphry Repton as the original designer of the park at Blatchards, the estate in which the titular Yellow Room is located. None of these facts bear any relationship to the plot, however. Though one character ends up "facedown among the cyclamen," it is a death by natural causes.

Could a single plant be a murder setting? The closest I came was the ancient Scots elm central to Tana French's novel, *The Wych Elm* (the title of the US edition was Americanized as *The Witch Elm*). The action is rooted to the back garden of a family's Dublin home and its tree, an aged colossus. The fissured trunk of the *Ulmus glabra* conceals secrets. Unfortunately, the elm, a silent witness to past crimes, must die to reveal them.

Specific garden elements sometimes take center stage in crime fiction, acting as settings and sometimes as titles. Take mazes for example, those complex puzzles of paths and shrubbery. One of them stars, unsurprisingly, in *Murder in the Maze* (1927), by J. J. Connington, pseudonym for Scottish-born polymath and chemist Alfred Walter Stewart. (And, as my eleven-year-old granddaughter informs me, a maze is part of the mise-en-scène for the closing, murderous episode of *Harry Potter and the Goblet of Fire*.) Crime writers have staged homicides in ornamental garden buildings—Patricia Wentworth's Miss Silver mystery *The Gazebo* (1955) is one of my favorites. Author Marty Wingate turned from decorative to functional architecture when her gardener-protagonist stumbles upon a murder victim in her client's toolshed in *The Garden Plot*. In *An Unsuitable Job for a Woman*, P. D. James did away with her victim in the gardener's cottage.

Garden settings can also shift a series out of a usual location or add descriptive layers. They offer series writers new places to describe and give their perennial protagonists a new set of problems. When Canadian author Louise Penny made use of a remote monastery garden as scene-of-crime in *The Beautiful Mystery*—the eighth in her going-on-twenty book series—she moved Inspector Armond Gamache of the *Sûreté du Québec* from the village of Three Pines, where his life and most of the plots are centered. In *Trick of the Light*, set in the village, the victim is found in a garden; its bleeding hearts and fragrant lilacs add a sensual, ironic overlay. A relocation can enliven a series, and a return home can comfort hero and reader.

Yet as often as gardens have acted as location for murder—the *where*—gardens and plants have also figured into the *why*, the motivation for the misdeed.

MOTIVE

Gardening Made Me Do It

Gardeners are motivated by many things, most of them positive. A connection with nature or beauty. The siren song of fresh produce or cut flowers, grown to match a personal preference. Memory can be a driver, a recollection of plants tied to a certain person or place. Yet anyone who has participated in a garden tour, entered a flower show, or discussed the degree of tomato ripeness with a neighbor knows that gardening can be a competitive sport. It's a short distance from ambition to compulsiveness, and one of the faces of compulsion is control.

PERFECTION MADE ME DO IT

The neatness of the gardens was almost oppressive.

—FROM "WEEDS" BY RUTH RENDELL

Picture a bright English summer day in the north Suffolk countryside. A village garden is open for visitors, part of a charity scheme to raise money for cancer research. It costs two pounds to gain entry. A London editor, Jeremy Flintwine, accompanies some friends—writers with whom he has spent the weekend—to the event. He feels out of step with the enterprise. The whole affair confirms his general dislike of the country.

Flintwine is not in any sense a gardener, nor do gardens interest him. While the rest of the crowd is done up in frocks and summer jackets, he wears London attire: a tailored shirt with dressy jeans. His Italian silk cardigan sports a red poppy that one of his hosts had picked by the roadside and placed in his buttonhole. With no way to avoid the garden gathering, what to do? He notes there are refreshments for sale. And a game is afoot for the event: find a weed anywhere on the property and win one pound. It won't be an easy prize, as the garden in Ruth Rendell's story "Weeds" is a picture of the meticulously maintained garden.

Rendell's taut prose makes it clear that the beds and borders are within the purview of a control freak. The lawn is billiard table-smooth; the flowers so perfect, they seem artificial. If you tend to the finicky in your horticultural practices, you may say, "Ahhh, a kindred spirit." While other visitors are in pursuit of a winning weed, Jeremy seeks a secluded corner to cadge a smoke. What he observes—both the scheming weed hunters within the garden and amorous affairs on the other side of the garden wall—confirm his attitude that country life goes beyond rural to feral.

Weeds are always uninvited guests, the party crashers of the garden, exposing killer instincts in most cultivators of the soil. Rendell uses these inclinations to stunning effect in "Weeds," though some of her weeds are classed with species *Homo sapiens*. For those of the plant kingdom, she is in the company of many other author-gardeners.

Of weeding the ragweed out of her snapdragons, Frances Hodgson Burnett, author of *The Secret Garden*, once commented, "It is necessary for me to control evil impulses which I should prefer to believe did not lurk in the depths of an apparently mild nature." She had murder in her heart. If this invasive member of the aster family is on a rampage in your garden, you will sympathize with her longing to hack through the bed, snapdragons and all.

Still worse for Burnett was pusley (*Portulaca oleracea*), what many of us call purslane. She found it even "more sneaking and creeping." In my garden, it disguises itself as moss-rose (*Portulaca grandiflora*), so sneaking is the right word. My husband eats the weed in salads, but it makes me lose my appetite after doing battle with it in the vegetable beds. Burnett's contemporary, Charles Dudley Warner, concurred. In *My Summer in a Garden* (1871) he waxed militantly poetic on a pusley plague. "My warfare with it has been continual," he wrote. "Neither of us has slept much. If you combat it, it will grow, to use an expression that will be understood by many, like the devil." (Warner was, by the way, a neighbor and sometime collaborator of Samuel Langhorne Clemens, aka Mark Twain, in Hartford, Connecticut.)

So, consider this a warning. A tidy garden is a wonderful quality, within bounds. Keep your penchant for control in perspective or things might go very, very wrong. This admonition is magnified in another lifelong fixation with a garden, a rose garden, in the aptly named *Deadheads* by Reginald Hill.

THE ROSE GARDEN MADE ME DO IT

It's just rather uncanny, this certainty of his that everything will be all right, that nothing will ever be allowed to threaten Rosemont.

—FROM *DEADHEADS* BY REGINALD HILL

Most murder mysteries move in a forward direction, from the discovery of a crime to the unmasking of the criminal. They are classic whodunits.

Reginald Hill's *Deadheads* runs the opposite way. The criminal sociopath is introduced in an opening sequence that may give you pause the next time you take up your pruning knife or floral snips. A black comedy murder mystery, the book plays the wits of Detective-Superintendent Andrew Dalziel and Detective-Inspector Peter Pascoe off the stealthy actions of the serial killer, Patrick Aldermann.

Aldermann would do anything to protect Rosemont, his lavish family property. If a garden can be defined as a hole in the ground into which one shovels money, then Rosemont is his personal money pit. His great-uncle Eddie had loved the estate and, above all, his roses; Patrick follows in his footsteps. He is a real gardener, knowledgeable and hands on. Roses are a demanding lot, and his phalanx of bushes, shrubs, and climbers is perfection.

When something or someone threatens Rosemont, they have a way of disappearing. Patrick Aldermann is always there, standing in the wings. When his great-aunt wanted to leave the property to charity, she had a heart attack before she could change her will. When his mother wanted to sell the place, the buyer died before the transaction closed. To fund Rosemont's upkeep, he needs to advance in his company—Elgood Ceramics, a big name in toilets—and his colleagues keep dropping dead.

Each of the book's chapter headings is a named rose variety—description provided—suiting the given action. When an undercover DS Dalziel "accidently" bumps into the suspect's mother, the chapter is tagged 'Masquerade', a vigorous floribunda. 'Daybreak', a hybrid musk, is for a chapter about an all-night stakeout. It is a horticultural flourish that, one supposes, Patrick Aldermann would appreciate.

Aldermann seems to care more about flowers than family. When he counts his 'Blessings', he is counting hybrid teas rather than spouse and children. Aldermann's evil is intrinsic, a sociopathic trait as natural, in its way, as the roses which carry the genetic mutation for continuous flowering. Perhaps something has turned off the guilt switch in his makeup. Could it be his garden? When *Alice in Wonderland*'s Queen of Hearts screamed, "Off with her head," she was processing through her rose garden.

If you've had enough pleas of horticultural insanity, the theme of "the garden made me do it," is played out in a cozier way in *The Darling Dahlias and the Cucumber Tree*. In this series, Susan Wittig Albert spotlights the garden club of Darling, Alabama, whose combined efforts crack many of its small-town crimes. Plants and gardens abound. In the series premiere, something buried in a garden motivates one strand of the twisting plot.

MONEY MADE ME DO IT

It is 1930. The small but enthusiastic garden club of Darling, Alabama, is in mourning for its founder, Mrs. Dahlia Blackstone, may she rest in peace. In her will, Mrs. Blackstone left her house to the organization for

its clubhouse, along with the lot it sits on. Her only nephew, who had been anticipating his inheritance, is crushed. Still, those were her wishes.

In Mrs. Blackstone's honor, the club members rename themselves "The Dahlias" and pitch in to recapture her beloved borders from the weeds. They rescue lilies, old garden roses, and "pass-along" plants beloved of gardeners North and South—iris, phlox, shasta daisies, and daylilies. When the membership considers the club's bank account however, the picture is dire. Mrs. Blackstone had left money to cover property taxes but nothing for a much-needed roof. With the financial shock waves of the 1929 stock market crash, fundraising is nearly impossible. Yes, money is getting to be a big problem in this charming little fictional town which made its debut in *The Darling Dahlias and the Cucumber Tree* (2010).

Like Pecan Springs in her China Bayles series, author Susan Wittig Albert's detailed descriptions of Darling, Alabama, are vivid. The town, population 907, is the county seat of the fictional Cypress County. It is a close-knit community nestled in the wooded hills between Monroeville and the Alabama River. Mobile, some seventy miles south, is the closest big city. The sounds of horse and wagon can still be heard along Darling's streets along with increasing numbers of automobile engines.

The people seem as real as the place. In her Darling Dahlias books, Susan Wittig Albert employs the garden club's membership roster to introduce varied talents into the mix. Dorothy Rogers, for example, is town librarian and a stickler for proper botanical nomenclature. She informs her friends they must refer to the cucumber tree in Mrs. Blackstone's garden as *Magnolia acuminata*. The artistic Beulah Trivette owns the hair salon. It is the hub of local news and gossip, though the local diner, managed by Myra May Moswell and Violet Sims, runs a close second. There is a bank teller, a boardinghouse owner, the mayor's wife, and more.

Two garden club members serve as the primary detectives in these chronicles. Verna Tidwell, the probate clerk, is naturally suspicious. Her job gives easy access to public records, and she is a voracious consumer of the detective novels and true crime magazines of the day. Elizabeth "Lizzie" Lacy, a legal secretary, writes "The Garden Gate" column for the *Darling Dispatch*, where she recounts the history of the seven sisters' rose. (A real-life

Southern garden writer, Elizabeth "Libba" Lawrence [1904–1985], wrote a gardening column for the *Charlotte Observer* for many years. The columns were collected into a book called *Through the Garden Gate*.)

Verna and Lizzie, with more help from the Dahlias than from the local sheriff's office, sort out some shadowy goings-on. A drugstore clerk, the blonde, buxom Bunny Scott, disappears. There is an escaped convict on the loose. As in many places across the country during the Depression, folks are hearing rumors about troubles at the local bank. Plus, someone keeps digging under Mrs. Blackstone's cucumber magnolia at the garden club's new headquarters.

If the greed-plus-garden-club theme attracts, try Louise Gazzoli's *Compost Mortem*, a parody of the horticultural mystery genre. As the title implies, it is full of word play and murder, plus a scam involving kink-free garden hoses. The town of Deer Creek seems too small for its two garden clubs, but the rival groups have managed to cooperate on the local mulch facility project. Unfortunately, a developer has targeted the site for a new residential project. Mayhem ensues.

A ROSE MADE ME DO IT

In English as well as many other languages, envy is green. Shakespeare gave jealousy green eyes, as in "green-eyed monster," not once but twice, in *Othello* and *The Merchant of Venice*. Plants, saturated with chlorophyll, infect many with acquisitiveness, sometimes to the point of murderous intent.

Plant lust is a guilty secret among gardeners, whether tending one hundred square feet or one hundred acres. An Internet comic making the rounds a few months ago showed a gardening group at a rally. One person chants, "Who are we?" "GARDENERS!" the crowd yells in return. "What

do we want?" "ALL THE PLANTS!"
"Where will we put them?" "WE DON'T
KNOW!" To have the latest thing, a flower
that blooms in no one else's garden, seems
downright irresistible. Plant breeders want
to scratch that itch, to discover or engineer
a variety and hit it big in the nursery market.
It might be something blue.

Children may chant, "Roses are red;
violets are blue," but the desire for blue does
not end with the modest *Viola*. Pursuits of a blue tulip or a blue dahlia have
gone on for centuries. But more than any other flower, a blue rose has been
the holy grail. That quest has mostly taken the form of hybridizing: taking
the pollen from rose A and fertilizing rose B, and so on and so on. People
have also used less traditional methods to turn rose petals blue, from food
coloring and spray paint to splicing the gene for delphinidin pigment into
the rose chromosome. The results have been interesting but alien. In *The
Blue Rose*, author Anthony Eglin starts off with a different premise, an
accidental discovery of a rosebush with cerulean blue blooms sets off a
deadly race for ownership rights. As one of his characters explains, "Any
fool would trade his left toe for a blue rose—it's worth a potential fortune.
Worldwide, twenty-five billion dollars are spent on cut flowers annually,
one fifth of that on roses."

The first plant patent was for a rose. Henry F. Bosenberg, a nurseryman
from New Brunswick, New Jersey, applied for it under a newly minted
law: the United States Plant Patent Act of 1930. His invention was not a
widget like Edison's lightbulb, but a living thing—a vigorous climbing
rose that he called 'New Dawn'. Bosenberg argued that its uniqueness was
its ever-blooming habit; one could enjoy its champagne-colored blooms

not only in June, but across the growing season. The Patent Office agreed and, on August 18, 1931, issued Plant Patent 1, the first of many intended to provide financial incentives and protections for plant breeders. Bosenberg could earn royalties on every 'New Dawn' sold until the patent expired. There have been some big wins: the 'Knock Out' rose, introduced in 2000, comes to mind. But like many laws, the Plant Patent Act has also had unintended consequences, including the attitudes portrayed—hopefully in exaggerated form—in *The Blue Rose*.

What if hybridization trials, conducted by two amateurs during the 1940s, yielded a truly blue rose? It is not an everyday blue, but the superlative shade of a fine sapphire. The blooms are fragrant, the size of tennis balls. Through time and circumstance, the plant is forgotten, overlooked in a garden in Wiltshire. That is the question that animates Eglin's novel.

The Parsonage, a rundown period house on a two-acre property, attracts buyers Kate Sheppard, a gardener and antiques dealer, and her architect husband. Early in the plot, Kate discovers the rosebush with sapphire blooms in a corner of the unkempt garden. She contacts Lawrence Kingston, retired professor of botany for the University of Edinburgh and renowned rose expert. He verifies their find, and they have visions of sugarplum riches. So does everyone else who gets wind of the blue rose.

If you are looking to learn about roses, you'll be delighted with *The Blue Rose*. (Anthony Eglin is an enthusiastic rosarian and active in the American Rose Society.) You will learn about the genetics of roses through Kate's perusal of Dr. Kingston's compendium *The Ultimate Rose Book*. When their nursery-owner friend arrives to propagate the rose before it is transplanted, get ready for detailed instructions on how to make new plants from cane cuttings.

Throughout the intricate narrative, you'll meet an American capitalist who is head of Baker-Reynolds Roses, an acquisitive Japanese collector with deep pockets, and a broker willing to do anything to make the deal. Throw in coded garden journals and a Bletchley Park connection for good measure.

The motive is clear. Everyone wants to own the blue rose, and someone is willing to kill for it. But roses are not the only plants to inspire murderous motivations. In *Death in Kew Gardens*, one of Jennifer Ashley's "Below Stairs" mysteries set in Victorian London, a rare variety of tea plant from China motivates two murders at the Royal Botanic Gardens, Kew. And then, there is the famed and coveted orchid.

AN ORCHID MADE ME DO IT

As Nero Wolfe would attest, the orchid holds many in its thrall. Charles Darwin would concur. After *On the Origin of Species*, he wrote an involved treatise called *On the Various Contrivances by Which British and Foreign Orchids Are Fertilized by Insects.* Sales might have improved if his publisher had given it the title *Everything You Always Wanted to Know About Orchid Sex* (*But Were Afraid to Ask)*. The mechanics of orchid pollination offer a mind-bending array of adaptations for getting pollen from the male parts of one plant to female parts of another. This may be the reason orchids have spawned so much scientific study, true crime (famously, *The Orchid Thief* by Susan Orlean), and detective fiction.

When I came across James Hadley Chase's *No Orchids for Miss Blandish* (1939), I hoped that I'd uncovered an example of horticultural hard-boiled. As a subgenre, hard-boiled crime writing is a city punk. Rather than the pastoral, though frequently deadly, country life portrayed by Agatha Christie and her cohort, writers like Dashiell Hammett took off from the gangsters and crime news of urban America. They created a class of tough guy heroes—all men—with their own moral ambiguities and their own

language: a plant is a spy, lettuce is paper money, slugs are bullets, and clip joints have nothing to do with pruning. Hard-boiled novels are violent and so dark that plants rarely grow there.

James Hadley Chase, one of the many pen names for British writer René Brabazon Raymond, wrote his two gritty orchid books in the late 1930s and '40s. Unfortunately, *No Orchids for Miss Blandish* contains no mention of orchid, singular or plural, in the body of the text, though a red carnation and a bouquet of roses have brief walk-ons. Nor does its sequel, *The Flesh of the Orchid* (1948). Instead, the word "orchid" is an indicator of class and gender, a stand-in for the socialite victim, her wealth, and her vulnerability.

There is one famous orchid scene in Raymond Chandler's *The Big Sleep*. Detective Philip Marlowe visits the West Hollywood mansion of a prospective client. (I can't help picturing Humphrey Bogart in the 1946 Warner Brothers film.) The butler at the Sternwood mansion shows him into the orchid greenhouse. Marlowe's first impressions of the conservatory are intense:

> The air was thick, wet, steamy and larded with the cloying smell of tropical orchids in bloom. The glass walls and roof were heavily misted and big drops of moisture splashed down on the plants. The light had an unreal greenish color, like light filtered through an aquarium tank. The plants filled the place, a forest of them, with nasty meaty leaves and stalks like the newly washed fingers of dead men. They smelled as overpowering as boiling alcohol under a blanket.

General Sternwood, wheelchair-bound and ancient, grows the plants merely as an excuse for the heat he craves. "They are nasty things," he tells Marlowe, "Their flesh is too much like the flesh of men. And their perfume has the rotten sweetness of a prostitute." As a plot device, these "abominable plants" are a brief interlude, but foreshadow the book's sexual themes.

More recent mystery writers have taken up the orchid motif as motive, not as cultivated plants but as rare endemics in their native habitats. The hunt for wild orchids drives the plot in the first book by Canadian mystery writer Michelle Wan. *Deadly Slipper* is a story of sex and death in the Dordogne region of France. Locals, expats, and tourists interact like the complex workings of a forest of native and introduced species. More botanical than horticultural, the novel brings the reader into the mysteries of the world of orchid hunters.

The story begins with Mara Dunn contacting Julian Wood, a Brit who has long lived in France. He is a landscape gardener, expert on local flora, and author of *Fleurs sauvages de la Dordogne* (Wildflowers of the Dordogne). Dunn, an interior designer, has relocated to France to work and to seek information about her sister who disappeared in the vicinity twenty years earlier. In a junk store, she discovers her first lead in years: her sister's old camera. Its roll of film holds many photographs of wild orchids. Her sister Bedie was an "orchid freak," she explains to Julian:

> He thought for a moment and then nodded his comprehension. "Sure. Orchid fever. Gets in your blood. With some people it's an obsession, especially the tropicals. Fanciers spend big money on them. The field ones you get around here are free but, for my taste, just as addictive."

Orchids fit well with the sexual energy of the book. Julian explains the flower structure, especially that jutting lip or labellum. One of Bedie's photographs had captured the man orchid, *Aceras anthropophorum*. There's another of a tantalizing cypripedium, an orchid that Julian has never seen before. In English it is called lady's slipper, but in French, that language of love, its name is *Sabot de Vénus,* the shoe of Venus, or *Sabot de la Vierge*, of the virgin.

Wan uses neighborhood personalities as characters in her novel. Former nobility—also orchid connoisseurs—are in reduced circumstances and reclusive; their son is a shady character. There is a local orchid society, the fictional Société Jeanette, where Julian's rivalry with fellow orchid authority, Géraud Laval, is fierce. That Laval, a retired pharmacist, is also a mushroom expert, seems suspicious. But more than the people, orchids take the leading role, and lend the botanical brio to the story. They are the axis around which the plot moves. Whether they are the direct cause of Bedie's disappearance, the reader soon discovers.

THE LAND MADE ME DO IT

Seven miles off Cape Cod, Martha's Vineyard is, in fact, the location of an isolated population of *Tipularia discolor*. It is endangered on the island, though plentiful in many southern states. This cranefly orchid—which gives its name to *The Cranefly Orchid Murders* by Cynthia Riggs—has a topsy-turvy terrestrial lifecycle. A single oval leaf pops up through leaf litter in the fall, calling out a green and purple hello to the brown woodland. It spends the winter busy with photosynthesis in the sunshine of the open canopy while deciduous trees sleep through their dormant period. Then, like a mystery, the orchid leaf disappears. If the plant is mature, it pushes out a foot-tall brownish bloom spike in summer, timed for pollination by small cadres of nocturnal moth species.

Victoria Trumbull—ninety-two-year-old poet, long-time Vineyard resident, and the protagonist of Riggs's novels—is good at spotting these unobtrusive endangered plants. And it's a lucky thing, because these small orchids may be the only thing standing in the way of development on the land where they are growing.

The land. There is a rising tide of demand for this large tract known as Sachem's Head. A developer envisions it as huge houses for summer people. The town recreation committee hopes for a campground. One group has targeted the spot for its eco-commune; another is desperate to preserve it as open space. There is money on the line, emotions are running high, then some of the players start turning up dead.

Yes, there are murders to solve, but someone is also stealing endangered plants. Cranefly orchids around Sachem's Head start to vanish, then reappear, freshly planted elsewhere. Curiouser and curiouser. Victoria must sort out the smaller enigmas of family relationships, long-held resentments, and the botany of plant-specific habitat requirements.

SCIENCE MADE ME DO IT

A few short years after Edgar Allan Poe published his first Paris mystery, another American author spun a suspenseful garden tale driven by scientific inquiry. Nathaniel Hawthorne placed "Rappaccini's Daughter" (1844) in the northern Italian city of Padua. His choice of setting was deliberate; the city boasts a centuries-old botanical garden, the *Orto*

Botanico of the University of Padua. It dates to 1545, a time when scholars thought fossils fell from the sky. The Padua botanical garden was laid out as a circle set in a square, surrounded by walls and divided into quadrants. It was a living classroom for medical students when a healer's bottles were almost entirely filled with plant-based tonics. The ability to distinguish toxic from beneficial species was critical, as were preparation and dosage. What better way to learn than from the plants themselves? In Hawthorne's time, the *Orto Botanico* was the oldest surviving example of a garden of its type. It still is.

Hawthorne's story begins with a familiar trope: a stranger comes to town. Giovanni Guasconti is from the south of Italy, and he has come to study in this city long famous for its scholarship. He takes rooms on an upper floor of an old building. Once, it might have been a palazzo. When Giovanni leans out of his high windows, he takes in a lush garden in the courtyard below. It is the precinct of the neighbor, Signor Rappaccini, a doctor of renown who "distils these plants into medicines that are as potent as a charm."

Giovanni is something of a voyeur. The walled garden with its exotic vegetation and old marble fountain fascinates him. Presiding over the space is a statue of Vertumnus, ancient god of metamorphosis, venerated for the growth of plants and transition of seasons. Vertumnus, from the Latin verb *vertere*, signals change, plus *tumere*, to swell. English owes words like diversion and tumescence to the same linguistic roots.

From his perch, Giovanni watches the wizened Rappaccini—"this scientific gardener"—examining his plants with focused concentration. In the course of his surveillance, the younger man is struck by an odd behavior in the older, a behavior that would be odd for any gardener. The doctor avoids all plant contact:

> He avoided their actual touch, or the direct inhaling of their odors, with a caution that impressed Giovanni most disagreeably; for the

man's demeanor was that of one walking among malignant influences, such as savage beasts, or deadly snakes, or evil spirits, which, should he allow them one moment of license, would wreak upon him some terrible fatality. It was strangely frightful to the young man's imagination, to see this air of insecurity in a person cultivating a garden, that most simple and innocent of human toils, and which had been alike the joy and labor of the unfallen parents of the race. Was this garden, then, the Eden of the present world?—and this man, with such perception of harm in what his own hands caused to grow, was he Adam?

Enter Eve. Giovanni's attentions, sexual and otherwise, are aroused by Rappaccini's daughter Beatrice, the young beauty who tends the flora that her father shuns. Within the walled garden she seems innocent and nurturing, but insects, lizards, and blooms from outside the garden perish at her touch.

With the name "Beatrice" and the sculpted portal of the garden, Hawthorne cements the connection with the Divine Comedy and Dante's hell-to-heaven journey. Perhaps Giovanni should abandon all hope, or perhaps he should recruit Beatrice as his guide. Like many of Hawthorne's tales, "Rappaccini's Daughter" balances on the keen edge of good versus evil.

Professor Baglioni, a rival medical man at the university and an acquaintance of Giovanni, acts as Hawthorne's detective. It is Baglioni who stokes the young man's suspicions. Does Rappaccini value scientific knowledge over human life? Has he hybridized hyper-poisonous plants? Is Giovanni himself the subject of an experiment? And what of Beatrice? The climax of the story echoes *Romeo and Juliet*, complete with apothecary and a mishap with an antidote.

Hawthorne crafted a garden morality tale with science as the driver. It posed a question to every hybridizer who had cross-pollinated or grafted in pursuit of a better plant. Is it right and proper to tinker with Nature? Two-hundred-fifty-plus years since it was written and seen through a twenty-first century lens, it could be a parable addressed to all who are "fearfully acquainted with the secrets of Nature."

♦ ♦ ♦

Ruth Ware concocted her own menacing poison garden when she wrote *The Turn of the Key*, published in 2019. With a dash of governess à la Brontës and homage to Henry James's novella *Turn of the Screw*, Ware's novel is a harrowing modern gothic of a nanny position gone very wrong. That the nanny-narrator, Rowan Caine, is unreliable, we know from the start. The book takes the form of letters from Rowan to her barrister, recounting events in preparation for her defense. The charge: murder.

At first her new job had seemed too good to be true. So what if she'd be the fifth nanny in fourteen months? The pay was excellent, and the location would be an adventure after her cramped London flat. She would live and work at Heatherbrae, an estate in Scotland, taking care of four girls, toddler to teen, with the eldest off at boarding school. Her employers, forty-something in-demand architects, have thoroughly renovated the old estate house into a high-tech smart home. The housekeeper seems hostile when Rowan arrives, but she's dealt with worse than that.

The absentee parents check in via webcam. Sandra, the mother, has left an extensive instruction manual crammed with procedures, a binder with protocols for care of the children and use of tech, most of which Rowan ignores. Mostly things are fine. It is lonely though, and creepily still at night in the country, save the disquieting noises of an old house. The baby behaves, but the two middle girls, Maddie and Ellie, are beastly.

On a fine day, Rowan hopes to distract the sisters with an outdoor adventure. She leaves the baby in the care of the housekeeper and lets the girls choose the route. For once not crying or quarrelling, they lead her down a herringboned brick path to a neglected garden. The walls are high. Though the wrought iron gate is locked, the girls know a trick to opening it. They enter a strange garden, shrouded in plants. Too strange. Rowan's forehead breaks out in a rash after she brushes against the leaves of an overhanging shrub.

Frantic, Rowan calls the mother with questions about the garden. Sandra explains that the last owner of the estate was a chemist with a specialty in poisons. The garden was his testing ground for plant toxicity. Many of its plants were poisonous in the extreme, some from mere contact. Yew, laurel, foxglove, nettle, and monkshood grow together in the poison garden like members of a dysfunctional family. It had been locked up when his young daughter died after eating some berries she'd found growing there.

Family is the ultimate motive for Rowan's story, the sometimes-toxic relationships of parents, children, and, in this case, a nanny. Those relationships coil through this gripping book until the turn of the key on the final page.

◆ ◆ ◆

With motives established, let us turn to the ghastly act itself—the horticultural means of homicide. Even without plant poisons—to be dealt with further on—a cold-blooded killer can have a field day with the many tools of the garden.

MEANS

Dial M for Mulch

It is a truth universally acknowledged that gardening is a virtue. A gardener's work is outdoors, nurturing and ministering to plants.

Don't be fooled. Certain aspects of gardening can easily fall into a column labeled "vice." Among horticulture's dirty little secrets, one could kill or maim using common garden implements. The sharp blades of various pruning tools make handy weapons. Shovels, spades, and mattocks qualify as blunt instruments. Read a few labels on garden chemicals, and you may want to invest in a horticultural hazmat suit.

Consider, for example, every gardener's desire to exterminate select members of the plant kingdom. The targets will vary, depending on one's preference and place. For me, there are the over-enthusiastic members of the genus *Circaea*, enchanter's nightshade, which, as Beatrix Potter correctly pointed out, are neither enchanting nor a nightshade. The rampant biennial garlic mustard, *Alliaria petiolata*, at least has the decency to be edible when young.

Topping my most-wanted list at present is *Pinellia ternata*, an imposter that tries to pass itself off as the native aroid, jack-in-the-pulpit. I'm confident that *P. ternata*, with its arrow-shaped leaves and tiny spathe and spadix, is well behaved in its Japanese homeland. After all, it didn't ask to be relocated to my New Jersey garden. But here, it insinuates itself among the surface roots of every other plant. It multiplies at speed, forming miniscule subterranean offsets that foil efforts to evict it by hand. In the old days, before environmental concerns changed my habits, the answer would have been an herbicide.

The garden shed's chemical arsenal has long been a boon to mystery writers. Herbicides and pesticides—death to flora and smaller fauna—can also poison larger mammals, such as members of the species *Homo sapiens*. Reginald Hill employed them in diabolical fashion for *Deadheads*, and they figure into the Agatha Raisin mystery, *The Potted Gardener*.

WEED KILLER

Most murder mysteries deal with the sordid, but some slide into satirical. If you need light entertainment, try M. C. Beaton's Agatha Raisin books. They are fun and colorful, detective fiction's equivalent of zinnias. *The Potted Gardener* is the fourth in opus Agatha, a series that numbers over thirty books and has been adapted into a British television series.

Agatha Raisin is an unlikely English gardener. After a childhood in the tower blocks of Birmingham, the ever-ambitious Agatha worked her way to the top in the competitive world of London public relations. She built her own agency and, finding herself on the far side of fifty, sold it off. Her next

goal: retire in quiet comfort to the Cotswold village of Carsely, close to London,
but a world away.

M. C. Beaton, nom de plume for
journalist-turned-mystery-writer Marion
Chesney Gibbons, died at the end of 2019.
She grew up in working class Glasgow.
Later, as a reporter, she covered the city's
crime beat. Like her character, Beaton
transitioned careers later in life. Leaving

the fourth estate to take up fiction, she wrote over 150 romance and mystery novels. Agatha Raisin came to life in the early nineties when Beaton
had moved to the Cotswolds town of Blockeley. She drew on its charms:
honey-colored stone houses, an antique church, a central green, and
well-tended gardens.

Agatha is Carsely's abrasive "incomer." Her style and sharp wit strike
predictable sparks among the insular village denizens. Though she likes
a good meal, she can't cook, nor is gardening her strong suit. Gin is her
beverage of choice, and smoking is a habit she can't kick. Her high jinks get
her into trouble, but behind the bluster, the smart and inquisitive Agatha
is endearing. That's lucky for her. Carsely, like most villages of crime fiction,
has more than its share of homicides.

There's nothing like an upcoming open garden to focus one's energy.
Not long ago, my neighbor opened his New Jersey property for the Garden
Conservancy. In the lead up to the big day, he could be spotted outdoors
after dark, hard at work wearing a head lamp. In *The Potted Gardener*,
Carsely residents are similarly busy. They are getting ready for a village open
day. Residents will invite paying guests into their gardens—all proceeds
to charity—and compete for horticultural prizes. Who has the most

pampered peonies, the prettiest pansies, the best garden in the village? Mrs. Bloxby, the vicar's wife, will judge the contestants. Agatha, true to form, wants to win.

There's a problem, and her name is Mary Fortune. The newest arrival in town, Mary is elegant and well mannered. Her flower beds are pristine, her baked goods mouth-watering. No one has a bad word to say about her, to the extreme annoyance of Agatha. Adding insult to injury, Carsely's newest queen bee also seems to be taking over James Lacey, Agatha's own intermittent flame.

But there's something amiss about Mary. Underneath her perfect shell, she is adept at delivering quiet, poisonous barbs. When she refers to Agatha as "our very own Miss Marple," her implication is geriatric rather than clever. Harumph. In the garden competition Mary will be the one to beat.

Those who have ever put hand to trowel in a concerted way know that gardening is a process, not an event. Agatha has other ideas. She gets an extra-tall fence installed to block the view of her property. Under cover of darkness the night before the competition, the plan is to smuggle in a landscaper to install a bespoke garden. Shazam! Full bloom and picture perfect. A first is guaranteed. (Instant gardening is an enticing idea, one with pull for reality TV as well as Agatha Raisin—think BBC's "The Instant Gardener," or "Desperate Landscapes" on the DIY Network.)

Meanwhile in Carsely, a wave of garden sabotage breaks out. The Bloxbys' roses are ruined. Mrs. Mason's dahlias are trampled. Bernard Spott finds his collection of koi belly-up in his ornamental pond. The local policeman dismisses the incidents as vandalism until Agatha and James come upon Mary Fortune in her garden in an awkward position. She is quite dead. The autopsy uncovers the cause. "Someone poisoned her first with weed killer, then strung her up."

Plans for the open day move forward despite the murder, though Agatha's attention is riveted on solving the crime. Both her scheme for an overnight blue-ribbon garden and her detective work take some interesting twists. Everyone is a suspect in her book, from the green-fingered villagers to Mary's daughter, Beth. True to her personality, Agatha gets herself into several outrageous pickles seeking proof before she exposes the murderer.

And that instant garden? The contractor installs it in the wee hours before the event opens. The fence comes down, and the results are impressive. But sorry, Agatha. Someone has switched the labels on your plants, so your scheme is foiled. Disqualified for a blue ribbon, but top grades for detection.

◆ ◆ ◆

Weed killer also plays a part in *Strong Poison* (1930), the Dorothy L. Sayers novel that brought Harriet Vane to the attention of Lord Peter Wimsey. Vane is Oxford-educated, unconventional and a successful writer, as was Sayers herself. Lord Peter, the prototypical gentleman detective, is smitten. For a budding romance, their meeting place is awkward.

The book opens in a courtroom. The roses in a vase on the judge's bench are the color of blood. In the dock is Harriet Vane. The Crown accuses her of the premeditated murder of her estranged lover, poisoned by arsenic. As the judge makes his summation for the jury, he recounts the testimony:

> The prisoner, as she herself states, this time procured a tin of arsenical weed killer, of the same brand that was mentioned in the Kidwelly poisoning case. This time she gave the name of Edith Waters. There is no garden attached to the flats where she lives, nor could there be any conceivable use for weed killer on the premises.

As the jury retires to consider their verdict, everything and everyone is against Harriet Vane: evidence, the press, and public opinion. Everyone, that is, except Lord Peter Wimsey.

Strong Poison is Lord Peter's sixth appearance in the catalogue of Dorothy L. Sayers's crime fiction. He is the younger son of the Duke of Denver, debonair if foppish, with his monocle and Saville Row–tailored suits. He is impeccably served by "his man," the consummate valet, Bunter. The clock is ticking for Harriet Vane, with whom Lord Peter is quite, quite smitten. A hung jury and subsequent retrial give him time to investigate the facts in a fast-paced, intricate plot.

By the close of the book the players are back in the courtroom. The vase on the bench that had held crimson roses on page one now holds bright gold chrysanthemums. It is a happy suggestion that the book will end, not with Miss Vane at the gallows, but alive to tell more tales.

Sayers employs another tin of arsenical weed killer in her tense short story, "Suspicion." It is a reminder to use care in storing garden chemicals. Lock them up, even.

Mrs. Sutton, the Mummerys' new cook, has been a godsend. Too bad that she didn't have references, though her reasons—taking care of her widowed mother—seemed sound. Her tasty dishes and sweet, matronly disposition suit Harold and his wife Ethel perfectly.

Harold has been under the weather of late, ranging from a touch of dyspepsia to nausea and its consequences. Could it be Mrs. Sutton's cooking? His business partner makes matters worse when he goes on about an unsolved series of poisonings in the news. The suspect has been known to pose as a cook.

One fine fall afternoon, Harold goes out to plant the last of his bulbs. He grabs his trowel and bag of tulips, then starts rooting around in the potting shed for a kneeling mat.

When had he had the mat last? He could not recollect, but he rather fancied he had put it away under the potting-shelf. Stooping down, he felt about in the dark among the flower-pots. Yes, there it was, but there was a tin of something in the way. He lifted the tin carefully out. Of course, yes— the remains of the weed killer.

The stopper isn't tightly in place. From there, the action winds tighter and tighter, a mainspring of suspense, until Harold discovers the truth. A terrible truth.

TOOLS OF THE TRADE

A plethora of tools in a typical garden shed have been handled in heinous fashion in crime fiction. Take thirty-gallon lawn-and-leaf bags. In suburban neighborhoods around much of the United States, autumn is the season of ubiquitous bags: big, brown, paper bags. Gone are the giant leaf mounds and smoldering ashcans of my youth. They have been replaced by tidy rows of bags, lined curbside for Departments of Public Works to transport to municipal compost areas.

On occasion I have succumbed to the temptation to pinch a few of my neighbors' bulging bags for my own purposes. Dried chopped leaves are my mulch of choice. Even though I reside on Pine Street, there are, sadly, not enough trees of the genus *Pinus* to produce adequate pine straw mulch. To me, leaf mulch represents creative reuse of an ample, available raw material. With a small amount of electricity to run the leaves through my electric chipper, it also appeals to inclinations environmental. Goodbye shredded wood

mulch in plastic bags. Merely thinking about it gives me a self-satisfied—or is it sanctimonious?—glow of thrift and sustainability. Since reading Ann Ripley's *Mulch* (1994) however, I've rethought the part about picking up other people's bagged leaf litter.

Ripley's main character, Louise Eldridge, is a gardener-cum-writer after my own heart. She and her family have moved—again—this time to a woodsy Virginia enclave on the outskirts of Washington, DC. Her foreign service (read "spy") husband, Bill, has a new posting to the State Department. Before the movers have unpacked the van, Louise is rethinking their entire yard.

Like most organic gardeners, Louise likes leaves—living foliage on plants, dried leaves as mulch, ground leaves to fill and level the new property. Her teenaged daughter Janie is too embarrassed to ask the neighbors for the piles they are raking out of their woods, but when her mother suggests driving further afield on an after-dark leaf-collecting raid, she is happy to participate.

The next afternoon when Louise, Janie, and Bill set out to spread their leafy loot, they get a horrifying surprise. A few of the bags contain body parts. Dismemberment had been executed with an outdoor power tool, the chain saw, a process too gory for me or the author to dwell upon. Soon Detective Mike Geraghty is on the job, but Louise, a natural investigator, just can't leave the problem alone. Neither can her sixteen-year-old daughter, so it must run in the family.

The novel is a snapshot in time, written during the first wave of the women's liberation movement; the book came out in 1971, the same year the Equal Rights Amendment was approved by the US House of Representatives. One of Ripley's suspects is a model for the term "male chauvinist pig" and Louise is taking on a new career as a garden writer. She lands two assignments: an article on ferns and a second on bromeliads.

Horticultural murder mysteries offer tidbits on plant-related topics. When, like most garden writers, Louise acquires live specimens, the reader gets a thumbnail sketch of selected bromeliads:

> Her eyes rested on 'Snowflake', big pale green leaves speckled like a snake. Bold yellow flowers. She touched a leaf; it was cool and waxy. 'Heart's Blood', with its leaves that looked as if they were drenched with dried blood, and its flowers brilliant bloodred. *Aechmea recurvata* × *Aechmea pimenti-velosoi*, probably the rarest one of all, with its unreal cylindrical blooms in yellow, black, and orange. And then the delicate *Tillandsia cyanea* from Ecuador, not quite as fierce as the others. And, of course, the billbergia.

With words that conjure violence, venom, and open wounds, Ann Ripley has deployed a set of spiky, tropical exotics to foreshadow the book's climax.

The author and her heroine know their botanical Latin, though there was one blooper. Louise, learning about the specific body parts in the leaf bags, "vomited near a large *Pieris japonica* bush, then lost her balance and nearly fell into its thorny arms." Readers who like to ferret out horticultural gaffes will note that all *Pieris* are *inermis*.

If the chainsaw gore of *Mulch* leaves you yearning for something kinder and gentler, you might prefer Nancy Atherton's *Aunt Dimity and the Duke*. Put on something comfortable and brew a fresh pot of tea.

The female protagonist, Emma Porter, has spunk, plus talent in her vocation—computer science—and avocation—horticulture. The forty-something Porter sets off on a solo tour of English gardens. Through a series of unlikely circumstances, she finds herself at Penford Hall in

Cornwall, seat of the fourteenth duke. Said duke, young and handsome, is in desperate need of someone to restore his grandmother's chapel garden:

> Emma stared at the ghost of a garden. The shriveled stalks that shivered in the breeze held no bright petals or sweet scents, and the withered vines that stretched like cobwebs across the walls would never blossom again. The chapel garden was a tangle of decay and desiccation, yet it held with it the sweet sadness of a place once loved and long forgotten.

Emma's green thumb is put to work, the phrase a clue that both she and Atherton are American. Otherwise, Emma would have had green fingers.

It is a garden-themed mystery, romantic and supernatural. Emma finds true love. There are ghosts, Aunt Dimity among them. Here, no one dies of unnatural causes, though there is attempted murder-by-grub hoe in the walled garden. The ending will satisfy any reader who hopes for happily ever after.

◆ ◆ ◆

The same cannot be said of *Passing Strange* by Catherine Aird, which begins with a final ending for the local district nurse in the English village of Almstone. It is judging day at the summer's charity flower show, but judgment day for Nurse Cooper, one of the volunteers. A good sport, Cooper had donned a costume—turban and shawl—to work the fortune teller's tent at the fête. In the middle of the day, she has gone missing, much to the consternation of the event organizer.

When volunteers are striking the tents at day's end, they find her mortal remains under a tarpaulin. Inspector Sloan, like his Victorian predecessor Sergeant Cuff, is a rose grower, a hobby that gives him unique insight into the crime. The instrument of death: floral wire. A reel of it had gone missing from Mrs. Kershaw's garden trug. Sloan explains:

> The piece that killed Joyce Cooper had two ends. One end fits exactly with the wire still in the flower arrangement that Mrs. Kershaw did. There's a tradition in the village, I understand, that the winning arrangement is taken to the church.

"'Twas passing strange," as Shakespeare wrote in *Othello*. Just as strange, though nontoxic, is how the judges could have awarded first prize to the underfed, underripe tomatoes arranged on the paper plate provided by the exhibition committee. By the last act of this engaging book, that mystery is solved too.

🌢 🌢 🌢

Like Catherine Aird's floral wire, ordinary garden tools are put to extraordinary use as murder weapons throughout the mystery tradition. For a chilling short story with flower garden, gardener, and a menacing hoe, seek out "A Curtain of Green" by avid gardener and Pulitzer Prize–winner Eudora Welty. Other authors select uncommon implements. Take Rosemary Harris who, in *Pushing Up Daisies*, plants a *coa*, a traditional Mayan scythe, in her target's back. Ovidia Yu doubles down on garden murder weapons in *The Mimosa Tree Mystery*, a novel set in Singapore during World War II. Her assailant wields an ornamental rock, then finishes off the victim with a pole pruner. But pointy tools aren't a garden's only dangers.

MORE MEANS

Pick Your Poison (Plant)

Perhaps it's fatal attraction. A typical herbaceous border could serve as a living cross-reference for a dictionary of toxicology. So many murderous plants are lurking in the garden, it strikes me that nursery pots should come with warning labels. An ancient philosopher proposed, *Contra vim mortis, nos est medicament in hortis*: nothing growing in the garden can stop death. In the world of crime fiction, plenty of garden-worthy plants have caused it.

Say "deerstalker hat and pipe" and most people will respond "Sherlock Holmes." While Holmes's expertise in most areas was encyclopedic, his knowledge of botany was, as Watson once said, "variable," and his skills in practical gardening nearly nil. Holmes owed his variable knowledge of botany to his creator who earned it at a prestigious garden.

Arthur Conan Doyle entered Edinburgh University in 1876 to pursue a medical degree. One of his required subjects was botany, conducted at the Royal Botanic Garden Edinburgh. Three years later, a brief article appeared

in *The British Medical Journal* entitled "Gelsemium as a Poison." It was signed A. C. D., and scholars consider it Doyle's first work of nonfiction.

Gelsemium sempervirens, Carolina jasmine, is a lovely addition to a garden if you are lucky enough to live where it is hardy, or close to a greenhouse if you are not. A twining evergreen vine, it trumpets into bloom with canary yellow flowers, generally in the latter days of winter. Extracts are still used as homeopathic treatments for neuralgia and a variety of related ailments; its potent alkaloids are under study in pharmacology. For Doyle, a headache sufferer, the question was dosage.

His approach reads as Holmesian. "Having recently had an opportunity of experimenting with a quantity of the fresh tincture, I determined to ascertain how far one might go in taking the drug, and what the primary symptoms of an overdose might be." His experiment had a sample size of one: himself.

Fortunately for the history of detective literature, Conan Doyle did not build up to a lethal dose of gelsemium, and he eventually exchanged a medical practice for the more lucrative profession of writing popular fiction. He transferred his knowledge of plant poisons to his creation, the inimitable Holmes. Sherlock Holmes never encountered a gelsemium murder, at least not in his documented cases, though John Watson observed in *A Study in Scarlet* that his friend was "well up in belladonna, opium, and poisons generally."

Arthur Conan Doyle (1859–1930), inventor of Sherlock Holmes and experimenter with plant poison.

POTENT PLANTS OF THE
FICTIONAL VARIETY

In recent years, we've come to accept that plants communicate. Through its vast root mass, a quaking aspen can notify its clonal grove of imminent drought conditions. Maples send airborne SOS signals to warn brethren of approaching insect infestations. Mixed arboreal communities exchange nutrients through what some call the "*wood*-wide web," a forest version of a supply chain, comprised of tree roots and the filaments of mycorrhizal fungi. Though different from human interactions, these are social behaviors. More like humans, certain plant behaviors might be deemed antisocial.

Over the eons, evolution has delivered a conspiracy of plant chemistry. In addition to the lethal-when-ingested phytotoxins, discussed later in this chapter, other less deadly plants are still dangerous. Poison ivy is a master of disguise. Its leaf surfaces can be shiny or dull, its margins smooth, scalloped or toothed. It can snake along the ground; climb a tree trunk, telephone pole, or rock face; or stand alone as an innocent-looking shrub. While in general they won't kill you, species of the genus *Toxicodendron* can deliver a nasty rash if you touch any part of them, thanks to their urushiol com-

pounds. It's nothing personal. The plants are merely exercising their competitive advantage. Author Alan Bradley employs it to good effect in his first mystery, *The Sweetness at the Bottom of the Pie*, when eleven-year-old chemistry whiz kid Flavia de Luce distills the essential oil from poison ivy leaves to spike her older sister's lipstick. Don't mess with Flavia.

Other plants eat meat. That overstates the science a bit. While they do not chew, gulp, or poop, carnivorous plants do snare insects (and, less often, animal prey) with various lures. They pull nutrients from ensnared captives with the help of digestive enzymes, offsetting the lean soils where they grow. Regardless of their digestive capabilities, carnivorous plants appeal. Specialty gardeners cultivate choice bogs of pitcher plants, sundews, and similar alluring, carnivorous plants. Venus flytrap, beloved of children, is the celebrity of the bunch. Crime writer Ruth Rendell made good use of *Dionaea muscipula* in her short story "Venus's Flytrap" as a botanical doppelgänger for one of the lead characters.

Generations of writers have drawn inspiration from this peculiar flora. And as if Nature weren't brutish enough, authors have invented their own phantasmagorical mutants. From H. G. Wells in his short story "The Flowering of the Strange Orchid"—beware "its leech-like suckers"—to Howard Ashman's book and lyrics for *Little Shop of Horrors*, you will find armed and dangerous fictional plants. Lloyd Shepherd created a botanical serial killer for his historical mystery, *The Poisoned Island* (2013).

Shepherd used real people and events as the basis for his novel, specifically Captain James Cook's first circumnavigation, the South Sea voyage of the HMS *Endeavour* from 1768 to 1771. Joseph Banks, a wealthy young man, wrangled an appointment to the crew as naturalist; he would become the British Empire's most-noted botanist. On the trip Banks and his helpers collected specimens in many places, including the paradise island now called Tahiti. The men aboard the *Endeavour* were Satan to Tahiti's Eden. Taking plants, they left syphilis in their wake.

For *The Poisoned Island*, Shepherd chose a time four decades after that original voyage to commence the action. Joseph Banks is now old, wheelchair-bound, and running the Royal Botanic Gardens, Kew—he has also been knighted. When Sir Joseph sponsors another plant collecting expedition, the story moves from fact to fiction.

The expedition commissions a ship for the voyage and christens it the *Solander*. Its mission: return to Tahiti and bring back more specimens. The omniscient narrator observes:

> For Banks, the transport of plants from one place to another is an
> Imperial undertaking, the whole globe merely a market garden for
> the English, with Banks as head gardener and Kew as the hothouse, the
> place in which English horticulture is fused with British ambition.

It was colonial plunder, botanical-style.

When the *Solander* returns to the London docks, it is laden with leafy treasures. There are plants in pots and plants in barrels, the ship's cabins and decks fitted out as a sort of floating greenhouse. Its live cargo is transferred by barge to its ultimate destination—the huge greenhouse at Kew known as the Great Stove. Its dried specimens are delivered to Banks. (Herbarium sheets of pressed plants ensured that identification could be done, even if live plants perished along the way.) The captain is pleased, and Banks is pleased. Botanist Robert Brown, a real-life figure employed by Banks as keeper of his herbarium and library, is busy, as is John Harriott, an actual magistrate and the first head of London's River Police. Both become characters in what unfolds as a period police procedural.

For something strange is happening in the Docklands. There is a series of brutal murders, victims all crewmembers of the *Solander*. Stranger still, they seem to have died smiling. The motive isn't robbery; their pay is untouched. In the absence of scuttlebutt, evidence builds that there is a connection to a plant, an unusual plant that Robert Brown studies on his employer's behalf. Brown observes that the specimen is a close relative of breadfruit.

The author has invented this particular plant—a fictional species of the genus *Artocarpus*—but reminds the reader of breadfruit's sordid past.

The real Joseph Banks collected dried specimens of *Artocarpus altilis*, the true breadfruit, on the *Endeavor* expedition and brought them back to king and country. Here the story darkens. Breadfruits produce large, abundant, and starchy fruit, which British colonial powers saw as a cheap source of calories for feeding enslaved people working sugar plantations in the New World.

In *The Poisoned Island*, a multi-layered, sometimes paranormal mystery, Shepherd gives his invented species an extra punch. It is hallucinogenic and dangerously addictive, a macabre botanical lifeform that seems to be exacting anti-colonial revenge.

A similarly addictive plant is the subject of *The Forgetting Flower* by Karen Hugg, in which she proposes, "What if a plant could make you forget?" Not everything and not forever, but a brief respite from trauma or grief. If word got out, there would be a flurry of interest, both licit and illicit. Now, what if that plant were your secret?

The main character in *The Forgetting Flower* is a recent arrival to Paris. Paris! With the European Union and its rollback of immigration restrictions, Renia Baranczka can finally live her dream of *la vie Parisienne*. She leaves her parents and twin sister in Kraków for the City of Lights. Savvy at retail and experienced in horticulture, she lands a position managing an upscale plant boutique. Part of her unorthodox compensation package is reduced rent for the apartment upstairs. The location is superb, in the 6th Arrondissement not far from Saint-Germain-des-Prés.

Whether Renia will be able to continue living and working in this beautiful neighborhood is questionable, given her boss's habits of depleting the shop's small cash reserves. And there are the complications brought on by a potent, fictional plant in Renia's possession. It demands clandestine care. It grows under lights, sealed in its miniature greenhouse, and concealed behind a wall panel in the shop. To tend it, she must don a gas mask. Why she keeps this dangerous plant remains an enigma.

Secrets will out. When her friend and best customer, Alain Tolbert, sinks into a deep depression, she gives him a sample of the plant's flowers to alleviate his pain. The first crack opens in Renia's world when Alain is found dead. Did she kill him? When her sister's loser ex-boyfriend, an addict and small-time drug dealer, shows up at the shop, things go from bad to worse. The economic side of plants—from nurseries to retail store displays to the criminal distribution of mind-altering plants—play into the twisty plot. Watch for a gardener wielding secateurs in defensive fashion at the showdown.

Mystery writers have fertile imaginations when it comes to murder weapons, whether tool or taxon. Kate Khavari confessed that it was too much fun to resist concocting her own poisonous nightshade for *A Botanist's Guide to Poisons and Parties*; she called it the South America xolotl vine, *Solandra xolotum*. But as tempting as it must be for authors to dream up new mean, green, and toxic species, most have made do with the array of actual killer plants nearer at hand.

OPIUM POPPY (*PAPAVER SOMNIFERUM*)

Years ago, as part of the application process for a summer internship at a local arboretum, I had a head-to-toe physical, drug test included. As she was handing me a plastic container at the door to the lavatory, the nurse practitioner asked, "Have you eaten a poppy seed bagel in the past few days?" I must have looked startled. She explained that even one bagel's-worth of poppy seeds could alter the results of a drug test from a urine sample. The poppy seeds used by bakers come from the same plant from which opium is derived.

That the milky sap of poppies, particularly *Papaver somniferum*, contains naturally occurring opioids is old news. Healers as least as far back as Theophrastus in the third century BC documented its uses. Ellis Peters, you may recall, included poppies in her descriptions of Brother Cadfael's medieval garden and workshop. During the eighteenth century, the British East India Company dominated the opium market, establishing a monopoly on the principal supply from Bengal. The Company exported and, where necessary, smuggled opium around the world.

Opium was the basis for a slew of nineteenth century pharmacological products. In laboratories, chemists isolated naturally occurring opiates such as codeine and morphine, revolutionizing the treatment of pain. Druggists prepared synthetic mixtures: laudanum (morphine mixed with alcohol), heroin (morphine treated with heat and other chemicals), plus a vast hodgepodge of patent medicines. A wave of opium addictions followed.

In history and mysteries, opium quickly took on a criminal cast. The drug holds a place in the collective imagination, particularly for period crime fiction. Along with prostitution, pickpockets, impenetrable fog, and Jack the Ripper, opium gave Victorian London its sinister underbelly.

While Sherlock Holmes was a sometime user of cocaine, he did not, as far as we were told, dabble in opioids. Only a fraction of his cases—five out of sixty—involve lethal doses of poison, none of them opium. Doyle seemed to favor unnamed tropical poisons as murder weapons, but he made use of opium in other ways, such as sedating opponents with doses of the poppy extract in "Silver Blaze" and "The Adventure of Wisteria Lodge."

My top recommendation for an opium-centric Sherlock is "The Man with the Twisted Lip," among the first dozen stories that featured Holmes. Appearing in *The Strand* magazine in 1891, it draws Holmes and Watson to a London opium den, a principal setting throughout the story. Doctor Watson mentions Thomas De Quincey's *Confessions of an English Opium-Eater* in the first paragraph. De Quincey's sensational memoir, published seventy years before Doyle cites it, influenced Edgar Allan Poe as well. Opium use figured also into Charles Dickens's *The Mystery of Edwin Drood*, unfinished when he died in June 1870. Anne Perry followed suit in her mysteries *A Sunless Sea* and *Treachery at Lancaster Gate*.

◆ ◆ ◆

While working as a pharmacy technician in a hospital dispensary during the First World War, the newly married Agatha Christie got to know her poisons. As a writer, they became her favorite means of murder; victims in more than half of her stories succumb to toxins. When concocting a new plot, she often reached for opium or one of its pharmaceutical offspring in her pantry of poisons. Morphine was an ingredient in the deadly dose in *The Mysterious Affair at Styles*, the novel that launched her career and that of her Belgian detective. *Hickory Dickory Dock* and *By the Pricking of My Thumbs* are two others with opium in the mix.

Opium poppies also happen to be one of my preferred garden flowers. Come April, I am on germination watch, awaiting the appearance of the gray-green seedlings in blank spots in the border and thinning them to the strongest of the bunch. They face steady competition for space from the early season perennials, and I often intervene on their behalf.

The payoff is in June. Drooping oval buds rise on erect, wiry stems to unfurl with color-saturated petals, thin as superfine silk—thinner, according to the latest science, than the outermost layer of your skin. Their colors suggest rosy fingered dawns and wine dark seas. I've lost track of the varieties I've broadcast sown over the years, though I can still pick out the deep purple of 'Lauren's Grape'. With their variations in flower structure—single, double, dissected, powderpuff—they hardly seem illegal, and it's hard to believe they can be lethal.

HEMLOCK (*CONIUM MACULATUM*)

Lately I have been struck by the number of umbelliferous flowers in my garden. There are several hues of *Ammi majus*, an annual confusingly called Queen Anne's lace, despite its difference from the Queen Anne's lace (*Daucus carota*) that populates meadows and roadsides. *Orlaya grandiflora*, white laceflower, fills the gaps in my border and bouquets every spring, a froth of white that reminds me of spun sugar. For yellow, there are the golden alexanders (*Zizia aurea*), native to much of eastern North America, and for burnished brown, there is bronze fennel. If you widen your view to sweep in my herb garden, you can add coriander, dill, and parsley to the list.

These are all siblings of the carrot family, formerly Umbelliferae, now Apiaceae. There is something about the structure of the inflorescence—with spreading parasol ribs—that attracts my interest as well as the interest of swallowtail butterflies and their umbellifer-eating offspring.

One species I do not grow is *Conium maculatum*. Its foliage and flowers are equally graceful, but it earned its common name—poison hemlock—and its reputation early on. It is toxic in the extreme to mammals of all shapes and sizes. The classical Greeks used it as a plant-based form of capital punishment. Sentenced to death in 399 BC, the Athenian philosopher Socrates consumed a lethal dose of poison hemlock, underscoring the syllogism "if all men are mortal and Socrates is a man, then Socrates is mortal."

The seeds and roots of poison hemlock have especially potent toxicity, and it is the latter that Elizabeth George added to her recipe for *Missing Joseph*, book six in her series featuring Inspector Thomas Lynley and Detective Barbara Havers of Scotland Yard. In the story, a suspect has gathered, washed, and cooked hemlock roots, serving them up as a side dish of wild parsnips, a look-alike plant. One of her guests succumbs. Inspector Lynley muses, "It would not be the first time someone with a bent toward the natural and organic life picked up a wild-grown bit of root or fungi, flowers or fruit and ended up killing himself or someone else as a result of an error in identification." Was this a forager's faux pas, or something more sinister?

YEW (*TAXUS BACCATA*)

When I was growing up, I remember my mother warning me to never eat the berries from the yew trees growing like tall sentries on either side of the front door. It was a reasonable precaution, as the bright red flesh—botanically arils rather than fruit—surrounds a highly toxic seed. So please don't eat the taxus. Fresh or dried, all species and almost all plant parts are toxic in sufficient quantity. In Agatha Christie's *A Pocket Full of Rye*, one of the characters is done in with tea laced with an extract of yew berries. Christie described the scene as "breakfast with the Borgias."

Visit ancient churchyards in England, Scotland, and Ireland, and you will often find a massive yew shading the old burial grounds. Some sources suggest that the ecclesiastical connections with yew trees stem from Druidic sources, with original Christian churches built on earlier sites of worship. The dark trees are somber, fitting for gravestones and their reiteration of grief. They have been called the "tree of death." Yet being long lived and evergreen, they also point to eternal life.

For all that, yews make lovely offsets to color-filled flower beds. Yews can be sculpted into topiary, as at Levens Hall, or clipped into cones, as in Hampton Court's Privy Garden. A solid hedge of yew is the backdrop for the seasonal walk at New York Botanical Garden where I bring my students every spring to reinforce identification characteristics of early bulbs. Yew is also the source of *Taxol*, one of the most prescribed chemotherapies for breast cancer patients. Now a synthetic, it was first derived from the Pacific yew, another potent species in the same genus.

FOXGLOVE (*DIGITALIS PURPUREA*)

For years, spires of pink and white foxglove have added spring verticals to most of my garden, from full sun beds to shady nooks. A biennial, it spreads at random each year, an element of chance punctuating my so-called planting design. The bumblebees forage nectar and pollen from its finger-like florets—think "digit" for *Digitalis*. Whole plants are abuzz with their efforts.

Digitalis purpurea, when ingested by humans, has two faces: angel or assassin. Preparations of foxglove have long been used to treat cardiac problems, though they have fallen out of favor. In the years when Agatha Christie was learning about pharmacology, many Brits were collecting leaves of wild and cultivated foxglove to address shortages of digoxin, a cardiac drug manufactured in Germany. Women and children sent thousands of pounds of leaves to local processing plants to be made into treatments for sick and wounded soldiers during the Great War. That effort was copied in the United States when America entered the conflict in 1917.

In sufficient quantity, foxglove can be fatal. Thus, it makes frequent appearances as deadly doses in crime fiction, and foxglove was one of Christie's

favorites. In her short story "The Herb of Death," Miss Marple's friend Dolly Bantry recounts an unfortunate dinner party. Foxglove leaves had been substituted for sage in the duck stuffing. Everyone served had suffered some ill effects. Oddly, only one guest was, well, a sitting duck. The questions of how, why, and whodunit are the subjects of the remainder of the story. *Postern of Fate*, the last of Christie's Tommy and Tuppence Bereford books and the last novel she wrote, recycles the digitalis device with foxglove leaves in a salad.

Foxglove has been a reliable favorite for mystery writers for decades. Dorothy L. Sayers, a great admirer of Christie, employed a pharmaceutical preparation of foxglove as the murder weapon in her Lord Peter Wimsey mystery, *The Unpleasantness at the Bellona Club*. It is unpleasant indeed when General Fentiman is found stone cold dead at the Club. Even more unpleasant when his heirs start bickering over the terms of his surprisingly substantial legacy. When the postmortem reveals a massive dose of digitalin, the questions are not only who, but how had it been administered. In his brandy? His pills? His mouthwash!?! For insights into the process of extracting this alkaloid ($C_{36}H_{56}O_{14}$) from foxglove leaves in a home laboratory, turn to *The Weed That Strings the Hangman's Bag* and eleven-year-old chemist Flavia de Luce. By the way, Flavia is detective rather than suspect, though she has an unusual penchant for poisons.

CASTOR BEAN (*RICINUS COMMUNIS*)

My flower garden hugs the house, occupying the only sunny swathe available. It is as packed as the New York City subway at rush hour. As a result, there is only space for one giant annual each year, shoehorned between the enormous perennial sunflower, *Helianthemum* 'Lemon Queen', and a vigorous stand of *Vernonia gigantea*, the ironweed whose specific epithet hints at its size. Sometimes I choose a dahlia to fill the spot or one of the giant zinnia cultivars, but often a plant from the genus *Ricinus* gets the nod.

Castor bean (*Ricinus communis*) makes a statement in my garden with its nine-foot tower of foliage and firework display of bloom, but its seeds can stop people in their tracks in other ways too. Saint or slayer? It depends on how its seeds are handled. Processed oil from the seeds contains useful triglycerides used as food additives, industrial coatings, and the traditional purgative, castor oil. The seeds also contain *ricin,* a poison that, in purified form, is deadlier than rattlesnake venom. It made headlines in 1978 when the BBC journalist Georgi Markov was poisoned by a passerby on a London street with a ricin-injecting umbrella. Since that real-life Cold War incident, many fiction writers have ripped the deadly use of ricin from those headlines.

Ricin-laced caviar served at the British embassy in Washington, DC, eliminates Her Majesty's ambassador to the United States in Margaret Truman's *Murder on Embassy Row*, part of her Capital Crimes series. (Truman, daughter of former President Harry S. Truman, had plenty of experience at embassy shindigs. For her mysteries, she had authorial assistance from ghostwriter Donald Bain.) Canadian mystery writer Charlotte Macleod used it in *Trouble in the Brasses*, an orchestral mystery in which garden-grown castor bean composes a dirge for a French horn player. In *Jerusalem Inn*, Martha Grimes substituted castor oil seeds for espresso beans atop glasses of after-dinner sambuca. It's a perfect ploy, since shiny round *Ricinus* seeds must be chewed or otherwise nicked to release

their toxins. Truth be told, the castor bean seeds I've planted are way too large to pass for espresso.

So, with little danger that I'd accidentally use them in the kitchen, the leaves of red cultivars like 'Carmencita' will continue to be among my signature specimen plants.

MONKSHOOD (*ACONITUM*)

All monkshoods are lethal, though some are more lethal than others. Regardless of species, whether one of the typical garden monkshoods regularly displayed in my local nurseries for fall planting (*Aconitum napellus* or *A. carmichaelii*) or one of the more unusual types from a specialty supplier, I don't recommend planting any of them near your vegetable patch.

One wouldn't want to mistake the lovely blue flowers for an edible bloom like borage or its leaves for a salad green. If this seems improbable, you might peruse "This Really Happened," a column on the website poison.org. There is good reason monkshood is also called queen-of-poisons. The concentration of the alkaloid *aconitine* in monkshood roots is especially high. Agatha Christie, the so-called Queen of Crime, had her

murderer substitute dried monkshood root for a prescription sedative in *4:50 from Paddington*. Instead of dropping off, the wakeful victim dropped dead.

Its usual common name—monkshood—is a nod to the shape of the flower. Its five sepals, the largest of which forms the upper hood, bear striking similarity to the cowl of a monk's habit. To me they look somewhat petulant, if not penitent. Ellis

Peters could not resist calling one of her Brother Cadfael books *Monk's Hood*, even though it was a spoiler alert in the form of a title. A less frequent moniker, devil's helmet, emphasizes the plant's one-way ticket to the afterlife.

Bring a taster along if you sit down to a repast prepared by a Martha Grimes chef. Grimes, an American writer best known for her twenty-five Richard Jury mysteries, favored lacing foodstuffs with monkshood. In various plots she disguised its pulverized roots, in moist form and dry, as items for the table such as horseradish and artificial sweetener.

Along a similar vein, one of my top mysteries featuring monkshood is Irish writer Sheila Pim's *Common or Garden Crime*. It is set in the picturesque hamlet of Clonmeen during the Second World War. The protagonist, Lucy Bex, is an avid and inquisitive gardener. One can guess she followed her parents' footsteps into the garden, as Lucy's widowed brother and housemate, Linnaeus, bears the name of the eighteenth-century Swedish naturalist who devised our modern system of botanical nomenclature. The inhabitants of Clonmeen are preparing for that typical village affair, the flower show. One of Lucy and Linnaeus's neighbors cultivates *Aconitum ferox*, an uncommon monkshood. Keep your eyes on that plant, and should you wake up and find yourself a character in the book, *don't eat anything*.

Fans of *Midsomer Murders*, the long-running detective show produced by Britain's ITV, may remember the episode entitled "Garden of Death." Villagers are aghast. A memorial garden on the grounds of the local manor house is about to be razed to make way for a tea shop. Members of the manor house family, in residence at the stately home, start dropping like proverbial flies. One of them is poisoned, succumbing to pasta well seasoned with aconite. This ninety-minute episode logs a body count of four, including one historical murder unearthed along the way. According to the fan-wiki for *Midsomer Murders*, that's about average for a brief interlude in the scenic but deadly village of Midsomer Deverell.

RHUBARB (*RHEUM RHABARBARUM*)

While researching this book, I faced some categorization difficulties. Should I include crime fiction with a focus on agriculture rather than horticulture? If so, Marcia Rendon's North Dakota mystery *Murder on the Red River*, about the North Dakota grain belt, and Attica Locke's *The Cutting Season*, about Louisiana sugar cane, would have made the cut. They are well crafted, with contemporary relevance and historic roots. Fitting them under a gardening umbrella seemed too much like cheating, but when I came across a murder-by-rhubarb mystery, I couldn't resist.

Unlike many who relegate rhubarb to the vegetable bed, mine is front and center in the flower garden. Its red stems and gargantuan leaves are eye catching, and its later inflorescence adds substance to the border. An antique rose, the crimson 'Madame Isaac Pereire' climbs the white trellis behind it, and it is surrounded by self-sowing annuals that set off its hues: blue forget-me-nots, pink cleome, and tall azure ageratum, among others. Since delving into crime fiction, I have a gained new respect for my rambunctious rhubarb.

Rhubarb is officially classified as neither vegetable nor flower, but as a fruit. When it arrived in the American colonies with Benjamin Franklin in 1770, Poor Richard thought he was giving it to his friend, nurseryman John Bartram, to grow as a medicinal. How it morphed into something nicknamed "pie plant" is lost to history. It was officials of the United States Customs Service who classified it with fruits in 1947, since import duty was lower than on vegetables. At the time, no one thought of it as a murder weapon.

Dessert eaters generally divide into two camps: rhubarb-lovers or -haters. The latter need not fear. But for rhubarb devotees like me, if a longtime enemy appears out of the blue with a rhubarb dessert, think twice before you reach for a piece. While rhubarb stems are perfectly safe, its leaves are relatively high in problematic compounds known as anthrone glycosides. Consume enough leaves, and kidney and heart failure will result. Boiling down rhubarb leaves to concentrate the toxins might furnish an ingredient in a perfect crime, particularly if the bitter concoction is masked by other flavors.

Rhubarb at its most innocent is notoriously tart, requiring a heavy hit of sugar or sweeter fruits to balance the taste in recipes. Thus, the classic pairing of strawberries and rhubarb was born. *Strawberry Yellow* by Naomi Hirahara explores a darker relationship between these two fruits.

Watsonville, California, a real place with a real history of agriculture, provides the setting and social milieu for the book. In the late 1800s, many Japanese immigrants, *Issei*, settled to make a life on the rich land of the Pajaro Valley. Strawberry production became a specialty of theirs, first as sharecroppers, then as independent farmers, finally as cooperatives.

Mas Arai, the fictional detective of seven of Hirahara's mysteries, was born in Watsonville. As a young boy his parents sent him to Japan, to the family town of Hiroshima, for his education. There, he survived the atomic bomb. The Japanese American farmers who hired him upon his post-war return to the States had spent the previous years in US government internment camps. Only a few had managed to hold on to their land.

Fast forward to the present. Mr. Arai, who runs a residential gardening business in Los Angeles, returns to his birthplace once more. He comes back for the funeral of his cousin, Shug Arai, who had been a key member of the "Sugarberry" strawberry cooperative. Mas gets swept up investigating Shug's death. The strawberry business is becoming chaotic: pending announcements of breakthrough varieties, betrayals over breeding rights, and an outbreak of a strawberry disease called "lethal yellows." More than strawberries are dying. Be on the lookout for the rhubarb. (Naomi Hirahara told me she has only eaten rhubarb pie once. Not a fan.)

◆ ◆ ◆

Rarer plants also make appearances as murder weapons. In Peter Pringle's novel *Day of the Dandelion*, an Oxford University researcher is murdered with a sliver of rosary bean (*Abrus precatorius*). This climbing vine, native to India and southeast Asia, needs tropical conditions to flower, limiting it in the continental United States to South Florida where it is now considered invasive. Purple blossoms are followed by pea-like pods that open to display brilliant scarlet seeds. They're killers. Pringle's mystery stars Arthur Hemmings, PhD. When he isn't working as a botanist at the Royal Botanic Gardens, Kew, Hemmings is undercover, running clandestine operations for the Office of Food Security. Think of him as a plant-savvy James Bond. Double-O botany.

Many other garden plants have been plucked by mystery writers for their poisonous properties. Lily-of-the-valley shows up in Anne Perry's *Weighed in the Balance* and the finale of the fourth season of *Breaking Bad*, "Face Off."

 Daphne du Maurier builds suspense with laburnum growing in the Italian and English gardens of *My Cousin Rachel*. A range of kin in the *Solanaceae* family—the stately brugmansia and its weedy cousins, datura and belladonna—have been weaponized in Rita Mae Brown's garden-centric *Furmidable Foes*, Christie's *A Caribbean Mystery*, and Cynthia Riggs's *Deadly Nightshade*.

Whether the murder weapon is as obvious as pruning shears or as illusory as a poison, the detective still needs proof. And the path to that proof is the clues. Linguistically, "clue" is related to *cliewen*, an old English word for a ball of twine. It can be something one follows—think of Theseus in the labyrinth—as well as something one uses for trellising plants. Flowers, seeds, and other garden elements appear as key clues in crime fiction, crumbs of information marking the trail of the miscreant.

CLUES

Green Evidence or Red Herrings?

When writer and American art critic Willard Huntington Wright embarked on a mystery sideline, he assumed the pseudonym S. S. Van Dine. I was excited, as you might surmise, to find one of his twelve Philo Vance novels: *The Garden Murder Case*. A promising clue, but the book turned out to be about a person with the surname Garden, not about *gardening*. A dead end.

Clues are a fixture of the detective genre. In his "Twenty Rules for Writing Detective Stories," Van Dine listed first, "The reader must have equal opportunity with the detective for solving the mystery." According to his credo, all clues should be stated, plain and simple. There, I disagree. I prefer clues to flow from the characters and action as part of the natural course of events. The clues are camouflaged, unremarkable until they emerge with the final solution. The writer is, if you'll pardon the expression, leading you up the garden path.

I liken the best mystery clues to the self-sowing annuals in my border. On this August day, the divas are floral giants like tithonia—an orange Mexican sunflower I start indoors from seed—and the cactus-flowered dahlias grown with tubers dug and overwintered from year to year. They are supported by an assortment of perennial phlox, asters, and rudbeckia. But tying the design together is an all-volunteer chorus of annual *Euphorbia marginata*. I call it snow-on-the-mountain, though I first saw it growing wild on Nebraska's rolling prairies. Its green and white bracts add an understated theme to my garden, more like the alto section than the soprano. Clues should likewise be understated but essential.

P. D. James, author of eighteen crime novels between her forty-second birthday and her death at age 94, knew the virtues of clues so mundane that they often go unnoticed by readers and characters alike. "We know in our experience that extraordinary coincidences do happen," she said in a 1997 National Public Radio interview with Terry Gross, "and they do, I think, very often in real-life investigations of murder. But somehow it isn't right in the mystery." Plants make for a perfect clue, as they are everywhere and yet an often-overlooked part of our world.

In 1999, two botanists, Elizabeth Schussler and James Wandersee, wrote a guest editorial for *The American Biology Teacher*. They were lobbying for education to prevent a syndrome they termed "plant blindness," an inability to recognize plants and their importance. People have a tendency—validated in studies of school children—to rank animals first in importance.

Plants are easier to ignore than animals. Members of the plant kingdom probably won't eat us, in contrast to "lions and tigers and bears." Plants stay put. We can't see the forest, not for the trees, but for the movement of birds and other members of the animal kingdom. When not in flower, plants are most often a shade of green or brown. They blend in, and our eyes and brains filter them out. Plant blindness complicates the work of conservationists and educators. For the authors of detective fiction, however, plant blindness can be a boon. Who would notice a scratch from a rose?

THE THORN OF THE ROSE

As we approach the end of *Sad Cypress*, Hercule Poirot visits the accused, Elinor Carlisle. She is in prison, awaiting trial for the murder of her elderly aunt. The outcome seems certain to go against the defense, meaning that Elinor will hang. Undeterred, Poirot interviews her again at length about the details surrounding the crime. In a hypnotic moment, Elinor recalls a minor incident. The nurse caring for her aunt had had a scratch on her wrist. The scratch, according to Nurse Hopkins, had come from a rose, trellised by the door to the lodge.

This puzzles Poirot. Something troubles him from his investigations around the aunt's property, something about that scratch from the rose that doesn't fit. When his little grey cells get working on a problem, give him room. His lack of horticultural skills notwithstanding, Poirot discerns, in this offhand remark about a plant, a glimmer of hope. He returns to the scene of the crime and considers further.

You see, the rose climbing up the lodge's trellis was the variety 'Zéphrine Drouhin'. It is an old garden rose, introduced in 1868 by its French breeder, and named for his wife. If you enter "thornless rose" into your search engine of choice, 'Zéphrine Drouhin' is the result that will pop up, with its deep pink, luxurious blooms. There is no possibility of Nurse Hopkins having

been scratched by the nonexistent prickles on the green canes of that rose. Counsel calls a rosarian to the stand and a key piece of the defense clicks into place.

Christie never disclosed how her Belgian detective learned about this Bourbon rose, but she knew about it herself. Did she grow 'Zéphrine Drouhin'? No evidence—circumstantial or otherwise—has surfaced to date. In my garden, it is, for obvious reasons, my favorite to prune.

FORAGING FOR CRIME

Unlike the 'Zéphrine Drouhin' rose, grown far and wide since its introduction, some plants offer specific locational clues. American ginseng acts as one such tell in Vicki Lane's *Signs in the Blood*.

With the scientific name *Panax quinquefolius*—who says botanists aren't poetic?—the plant has been dug for profit for over three centuries. French explorers in the 1700s recognized it as a close cousin to a revered medicinal plant in Asia. There was built-in demand. American ginseng is the yin to Chinese ginseng's yang, and it quickly outpaced furs as a principal export from North America to the Asian market. By the mid-nineteenth century, the plant was considered rare in the forests of Quebec.

Ginseng hunting remains a profitable business south to Georgia and across the Mississippi as far as Oklahoma. No surprise that its range continues to shrink, with overharvesting and habitat loss. Ambitious growers are attempting to domesticate it, but its requirements are demanding. Perhaps it is worth killing over.

The North Carolina ranges of the Appalachians—setting for *Signs in the Blood*—are among its preferred native habitats. When Elizabeth Goodweather, the protagonist, finds shriveled roots of ginseng in the victim's backpack, she hopes it will lead her to another clue: the victim's missing rifle. She begins to search for the plants—local ginseng populations—and people—"sang" hunters and "sang" growers.

Elizabeth, a flower and herb farmer, knows more about cultivated plants than wild. She turns to her friend, a local elder named Miss Birdie, for guidance. Unfortunately, ginseng colonies won't be easy to spot in the spring because it looks like many other plants, especially the wild sarsaparilla. "It's in the fall when them leaves turns that yellowy gold and that big bunch of red berries jest hollers at you that folks digs the roots to sell," Birdie tells her. People who harvest and sell wild ginseng aren't likely to share its whereabouts either.

Undaunted, Elizabeth follows the ginseng trail through hills and hollers. She encounters local characters along the way, both suspicious and benign. At home, Elizabeth sorts through the details of the case while hoeing her own garden. Miss Birdie's traditional plant wisdom helps finger the murderer. For another example of ethnobotany-based clues, let us look further west to one of Vicki Lane's favorite mystery writers, Tony Hillerman.

◊ ◊ ◊

In *The Wailing Wind*, one of Tony Hillerman's many mysteries, seeds help crack a case. Forensic botany is a scientific discipline within the world of criminal investigation. Samples from a scene, suspect or victim, might come in the form of leaf, spore, pollen or other tidbit of plant or fungal material. They can provide admissible evidence in court, generally offered by experts who work in well-equipped laboratories. (For a real-life read, try *Murder Most Florid*, a memoir by Dr. Mark Spencer, a botanist and crime scene investigator.) In Hillerman's novel, a Navajo shaman sets a police officer on a botanical trail that takes her from a dead body to the scene of the murder and ultimately to the culprit.

Hillerman had a sincere respect for native cultures. He spent his boyhood in Sacred Heart, Oklahoma, on territorial lands of the Potawatomi. His schoolmates in primary and secondary school were children of the Tribe. A decorated veteran of World War II combat, Hillerman became a journalist, reporting on crime and politics. In time, he rose to be executive editor of *The Santa Fe New Mexican*, and chairman of the department of journalism at the University of New Mexico.

The native people of the Southwest fascinated him, and he spent the last half of his life sharing their stories through his writings. Eighteen Hillerman mysteries star Joe Leaphorn and Jim Chee of the Navajo Tribal Police—sometimes solo and sometimes paired—and spotlight different aspects of life and traditions of the Navajo people. In an interview with *Publishers Weekly*, Hillerman said, "I think it's important to show that aspects of ancient Indian ways are still very much alive and are highly germane even to our ways."

One element of Navajo culture is botanical, using indigenous plants for everything from grazing sheep to performing rituals. In *The Wailing Wind*, Bernadette Manuelito, a rookie officer with the Tribal Police, answers a call about an abandoned vehicle on a dirt road near the Arizona-New Mexico border. It isn't only abandoned; there's a dead body lying on the front seat. Officer Manuelito notices the clothing of the deceased, covered with "hitchhiker" seeds, so called for just this ability to stick to garments. Among them, she recognizes chamisa, alias rabbitbrush, which doesn't grow at that elevation.

Bernadette "Bernie" Manuelito is a plant enthusiast, a botany buff as Jim Chee describes her. Her favorite uncle, Rodney Yellow, is a trained healer who uses plants in traditional rituals, an ethnobotanist in modern parlance. He taught her about plants as a child, so she takes seeds—samples from the crime scene—to him for advice.

He examines them and explains. The chamisa is welcome in wild pastures. Its white stems, grayish green leaves and yellow flowers provide much-needed salt for grazing sheep. Sacatan grass is overgrazed and scarce. The needle-grass is invasive. Even the goats won't eat needle-grass. These are all dry, flatland plants, so they probably all came from the same place, though not from where the truck was parked.

When Bernie mentions the spiked goathead burs lodged in the dead man's sneakers, she piques her uncle's interest. He calls it puncture vine; another common name is caltrop, a term shared with small metal devices that armies spread to puncture enemy tires or, in earlier times, damage horses' hooves. Goathead needs more moisture and looser soil than the rest of the seeds in her collection. Try an arroyo, he suggests.

Easier said than done, as the Navajo Nation covers more than twenty-seven thousand square miles with many such gullies. Luckily, non-botanical clues from the victim's truck in the form of a Zip Lube oil change sticker and receipt narrow her search range to under thirty miles. And the ingenious story proceeds from there.

Tony Hillerman was not a native American writer, nor did he claim to be. He was careful to acknowledge his Navajo friends and sources. With the stipulation of no publicity, he donated part of his earnings to projects and charities for the reservation: a water system, lights for a sports stadium, a retirement home. Among his many accolades—an Edgar Award, a Silver Spur Award for the best novel set in the West, and his term as president of the Mystery Writers of America—Hillerman was proudest of his 1987 designation as Special Friend of the Diné, the Navajo people.

• • •

For a series comparable to Hillerman's in its sense of place, move even farther west to California's Central Valley. That is the setting for Rebecca Rothenberg's four botanical mysteries starring a scientist: MIT-trained microbiologist Claire Sharples. As Claire's story unfolds in *The Bulrush Murders*, she is escaping a failed love affair in Cambridge with a new position at University of California's Experimental Field Station. In miles, she has gone about as far from Massachusetts as she could go, at least in the continental United States. The Citrus Grove Station is in the foothills of the Sierras, south of Fresno. Its clients are the farmers and agricultural workers of the San Joaquin Valley. In fact—as well as in Rothenberg's fiction—the land produces more than half of America's stone fruit and citrus crops as well as most of the almonds in the world.

Claire is more than qualified in the science required for her new job—researching controls, biological and otherwise, for fungi and mold infestations on crops. An expert in blight, wilt, and rot, her eventual transition into the festering world of murder seems almost preordained. What she lacks is expertise in native flora. That knowledge gap is filled by one of her colleagues: extension agent—and eventual love interest—Sam Cooper. Accompanying him on field calls and weekend hikes, Claire learns from him and about him:

> He rhapsodized over the flora of the alkali sinks: stunted, tough little plants only a botanist could love, plants whose common names—pickleweed, saltbush, iodineweed—reflected their hostile environment and their lack of charm. From time to time he'd remembered to say things like, "Agriculture could learn a lot from these halophytes," or

"It's amazing how this atriplex has adapted to these saline conditions," which hadn't fooled Claire for a minute. There was no practical reason for his interest; it was infatuation, pure and simple.

For Sam, the alkali-adapted plant life pales beside his favorite habitat, the marshlands, where he introduces Claire to bulrushes in their usual surroundings.

When a friend dies, presumably the victim of a motorcycle accident, bulrush and iodineweed are tangled in the spokes of his tires. The place his body was found was neither alkali nor marshland; earlier that night, his bike had been perfectly clean. Claire and Sam, both at the scene, find themselves stalking the killer on a trail marked by plant species.

Clues, however, can lead us astray. When ears of sweet corn started disappearing from my community garden, we were convinced some person was pilfering. That is, until a fellow gardener spotted a racoon at work. The critter climbed the fence, reached from fence post to cornstalk, harvested the goods, and absconded. Clever bandit. Our response: a "have-a-heart" trap. It seems that nineteenth century activists had a more involved strategy when it came to foiling a fox hunt.

WHITE FLOWERS OR RED HERRINGS

To throw hunting dogs off the scent of a fox, old-time animal rights crusaders deployed pungent, preserved herring as a canine distraction. Or so it is said. Salted and smoked for a long period, silvery herrings turn red. British cookbook authors call them kippers, but journalists—and later mystery writers—began to use the term "red herrings" as a catchy phrase for false leads. Red herrings are indispensable to mysteries, deliberate distractions

that set up surprise endings. Where's the fun of guessing whodunit early on?

A red herring in crime fiction can take many forms, including floral. A pure white flower leads attorney Nan Robinson on a wild goose chase in Taffy Cannon's *Tangled Roots*, a mystery twisted into Southern California's floriculture industry. Shane Pettigrew, scion of the powerful Pettigrew Nursery family, has developed a pure white hybrid alstroemeria. His triumph is short-lived; he turns up dead in one of their greenhouses. Scene-of-crime evidence fingers Nan's brother-in-law, Adam, as the killer. When the alstroemeria turns up at a competitor's propagation facilities, that seems to exonerate him. Or does it?

Using a white flower—the alstroemeria in this case—as a red herring is a subtle twist. The color white, beloved of brides and christenings, connotes innocence, purity, and fresh starts. Taffy Cannon isn't alone in her use of color in clues. When crime writer Martha Grimes employed hellebore blooms in *Jerusalem Inn*, she invoked white and black for contrast.

It is holiday time and snowy in the north of England when Richard Jury, a Scotland Yard superintendent, converges with his friend, the aristo-cratic amateur detective Melrose Plant (no horticultural significance). A village pub, the seedy Jerusalem Inn, provides title and backdrop, but not the main setting. Principal action takes place in a country house, Spinney Abbey, where Plant is on the guest list and Jury is his unexpected plus-one.

Nature cooperates, from the point of view of the plot. The Abbey gets snowed in, limiting the suspect list because, yes, there has been a murder. Still, no reason not to dine in style. The Abbey's tables are adorned with

bowls of pure white blooms. One of the guests, an avid gardener, had brought them as a hostess gift. These white flowers, generally known as Christmas roses, are also called black hellebores. "*Helleborus niger*, the black hellebore," remarks another of the party. "I suppose it's because of the root. That's black and extremely poisonous." The reader may suppose it is also a clue to the villain's identity.

FOOTPRINT IN THE GARDEN BED

The crime presented in the opening pages of Rumer Godden's *An Episode of Sparrows* may seem trivial—petty theft of a dozen buckets of soil from a central garden in London—but members of the Garden Committee are outraged. As residents of the fine houses around Mortimer Square, they are quick to blame the street children, "the sparrows," from the adjoining blocks.

The story takes place in post-war London, numb from the Blitz, a city of rubble clawing its way back. Two unlikely gardeners create an unlikely garden among the ruins. It is guerilla gardening before the invention of the term. This is a book of atmosphere, of plants and people, of life struggling out of waste spaces.

Lovejoy Mason, the eleven-year-old daughter of a singer and an unknown father, lives in a rented room in the house of an older couple who run a restaurant. Lovejoy's moral character is strong, if slightly warped by a mother who is absentee or worse.

Action commences when a neighborhood boy rescues a small item dropped on the pavement by a passerby. Lovejoy snatches it from the boy. To her disappointment, it is only an envelope of seeds—cornflower seeds. Worthless, but the packet nags at her with its printed picture of blue flowers, its itemized directions on the back flap. She starts to notice gardens of all sorts, and she wants to plant one. A planter box won't do; she wants a garden.

To garden, you need space, and Lovejoy finds it in a bombsite nearby. To garden, you need a few tools. The penniless Lovejoy is led into temptation. She purloins coins from an unlocked donation box at Our Lady of Sion Catholic Church. Ignoring pangs of conscience, she spends the money on a used gardening fork, prepares the soil, and plants her seeds.

Vengeance, divine or not, is swift. Her little garden is in the haunt of a gang of local boys who trample the seedlings out of spite. The gang's leader, Tip Malone, is tough but soft-hearted. He helps her relocate her flower bed to the ruins of a bombed-out church, but they need a quantity of good soil. They case the communal gardens at the center of Mortimer Square, break-and-enter, and make off with buckets of loam. It was

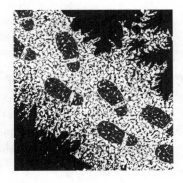

not a clean getaway. Exhibit A: a small footprint in one of the garden beds. And therein enters a police inspector, and the wheels of the criminal justice system begin to turn.

Inspiration for *An Episode of Sparrows* stems from an incident in the life of its author. After years in India, Rumer Godden had returned to London with two daughters in 1945; she needed a sanctuary, a place to live and write. On a shoestring budget, she took a lease on a tiny mews house off Eaton Square in London. The jewel-box property was impractical but charming, and it was close to the Square's park-like garden. There was a bombed-out church nearby. Godden filled the house with the best antiques she could afford—and many she couldn't—from the secondhand shops. A hired gardener planted her window boxes.

One morning two ladies called. Their purpose was not social, but admonitory. The soil in her planters, they said, had been illegally removed from the garden in the Square. "It was the first time I knew that earth could be stolen," Godden wrote.

Questions of ownership also figure into Naomi Hirahara's novel, *Gasa-Gasa Girl*. She sets signposts for her sleuth in a Japanese-style urban garden. In this book, I found Hirahara's interests dovetailed with mine.

A MESSAGE IN A GARDEN

I first saw the Japanese-inspired hill-and-pond garden at the Brooklyn Botanic Garden on a spring day when the cherry blossoms bloomed. *Sakura* it is called, a poignant time when the laden branches rain pink petals. We had come to see a living design by Takeo Shiota, a landscape architect from the early twentieth century who had created a garden near my home, a garden since vanished under a country club's swimming pool.

Born in 1881 in a village forty miles east of Tokyo, he studied landscape gardening and architecture in Japan. He came across the Pacific in his twenties, made his way to Manhattan, and established a successful Fifth Avenue design practice serving wealthy clients in the New York metropolitan area. His best-known project is the one I was visiting at the Brooklyn Botanic Garden, designed in 1914. Shiota died during World War II at a US government internment camp. The details of Shiota's life are their own mystery.

Two decades after visiting the Shiota garden, I discovered Naomi Hirahara had picked up the thread of his elusive story and embroidered it into her plot for *Gasa-Gasa Girl*, the second in her series starring gardener Mas Aria. Set in Brooklyn, the action centers on an old estate, repurposed as a museum, with a Japanese-style garden. The garden is about to be restored. While Shiota did not design this fictional garden, he reappears throughout the novel. Arai's daughter, a filmmaker, is researching Shiota's life for a documentary. His infant grandson is named Takeo. His son-in-law Lloyd, with sights on a PhD, looks to Shiota as a dissertation topic, though he is currently on staff at the museum as its horticulturist.

Unfortunately, the restoration project hits a snag. A body is discovered in the koi pond. The garden conceals clues, some past, some recent, connecting two families and two generations: patricians who paid for the garden and the Japanese gardeners who created it. Their lives intertwine on

a single property, alongside Mas Arai's complicated relationship with his own family. Ritual purification in the *tsukubai*, the traditional stone basin, seems in order by the end of the book.

Clues build cases, cases against suspects. Though one may hope that the accused gardeners one encounters in murder mysteries can present ironclad alibis, sometimes it just isn't so.

SUSPECTS
Shadowy Gardeners

In the board game Clue—Cluedo if you live outside North America—the object is to solve a murder, specifically the who, where, and how. Each player assumes the role of one of the suspects. It hit the market in the UK and the US in 1949, and though there were potential murderers named Colonel Mustard, Professor Plum, and Mr. Green—the Rev. Mr. Green in the British version—none of the six was a gardener. This is not the case in *Death in the Garden*, the second mystery and the American publishing debut of Elizabeth Ironside.

THE OWNER-GARDENER

In the first sentence, we learn that Diana Pollexfen has been acquitted of the murder of her husband, a Member of Parliament. If not Diana, then who: one of the circle of friends present to celebrate her birthday?

Someone on staff at Laughton Hall? An outsider? Did the jury get it wrong?

Action in the rest of the book is split, then and now. Two time periods—the interwar years and the present—reflect and distort, like an image seen through a prism. Diana remains on stage throughout, as do many of her friends.

The story is a stylish psychological drama that rides on surface civilities and dark undercurrents in an English country house setting. The house is called Laughton Hall in the twenties. Six decades later, it has been renamed Ingthorpe. Diana, now a great-aunt, is anchored to the place by its gardens. A view of the grounds gives glimpses of the past and the changes wrought since then:

> Beyond, sheep were already at their work of grazing, grouped pictur-esquely under the clumps of century-old chestnuts. The great-aunt had changed everything she could after 1925: her name, that of her son and her house; she gave up her profession, which she had defended against her husband during his lifetime; yet she did not escape from the past in the most obvious way. She did not leave her home. There was nothing to suggest that before 1925 she had much interested herself in gardening; afterward it became her life. Perhaps in the house and the garden lay her motive: her passion for them had already taken root, she could not leave them.

The great lawn, mowed into precise stripes, reaches to the ha-ha, that eye-tricking submerged boundary of English landscapes. Actor Dame Diana Rigg, in the role of the television detective Mrs. Bradley, once described a ha-ha as being "there to keep sheep and other riffraff out of the garden beds."

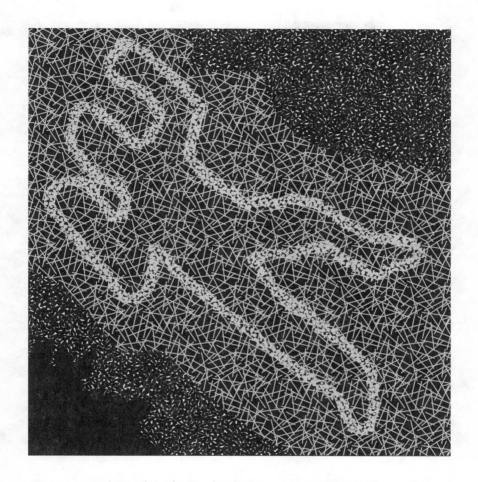

As you read *Death in the Garden*, keep your eye on Diana. Just as the house has more than one name, so does its principal character and prime suspect. At the beginning of the book, we meet a young, vivacious Diana Pollexfen who later morphs into the ancient relation who gardens with

such passion. In between, her husband is found murdered in the garden. Her adopted grandniece, a solicitor, acts as detective, piecing together the back stories of her great-aunt and her great-aunt's contemporaries, uncovering the many faces of Diana: professional portrait photographer, society host, possible murderer, and gardener.

Author Elizabeth Ironside has several identities of her own. Ironside is a pen name for Lady Catherine Manning, an Oxford-educated historian and wife of British ambassador Sir David Manning. The whirlwind responsibilities of a diplomatic spouse have suited Dr. Manning, and, in a sense, offered cover for what was for many years a secret identity as a mystery writer.

THE CARETAKER-GARDENER

Like Ironside, author Ruth Rendell did not hesitate to make a gardener the chief suspect in *The Crocodile Bird*, mixing a kinked mother-daughter drama with a tense thriller of murder, retribution, and gardening.

Liza, nearly seventeen, has long lived in isolation with her mother, Eve, in the turreted lodge of a gracious country estate, Shrove House. In Liza's life, there has only been Eve. Shrove House is Eve's personal Eden; she guards against any possibility of exile. As its manager, she oversees the estate with a single-minded ferocity. Its absentee owner is rarely in residence.

A silent gardener, Mr. Frost, keeps the hedges trimmed and the lawns mowed. Eve cleans the enormous house and tends the flowers and vegetables at the gatehouse. She plants the great stone tubs with geraniums, abutilon, and fuchsias. The front garden is full of flowering tobacco, scenting the air at dusk. Surrounding the cherry tree, Eve grows peas, lettuce, beans, and courgettes; gooseberries and strawberries are under nets.

Eve also provides Liza with rigorous home-schooling, Latin and Greek included, enabled by her Oxford education. Under Eve's direction, Liza reads selections from the Shrove House shelves: Shakespeare and Milton, and the Victorian novels. *Wild Flowers* by Gilmour and Walters is a help when Liza begins a collection of pressed plants. Luckily there are books, as the lodge has no television, no telephone, no car, and no contact. When Eve shops in the village, Liza stays home.

But something is rotten at Shrove House. Eve's occasional lover disappears suddenly and completely. In tandem with these events, Eve is inspired to expand her garden. The plant descriptions, while sinister, are exquisite, adding to the tension on which suspense depends:

> In the summer the solanum plant that climbed over the back of the gatehouse showed its blue flowers at Liza's window. Mother called it the flowering potato because it and potatoes and tomatoes all belonged to the same family. When she came up to bed that evening Liza knelt on the bed up at the window and saw, a few inches from her eyes, the death's-head moth, immobile and with its wings spread flat, on one of the solanum leaves.

The question is not whether Eve will be found out. That question is settled on the first page of the book. Rather, we wonder what will Liza do? With her unusual upbringing, will the sins of the mother be taken up by her daughter?

THE JOBBING GARDENER

In Ngaio Marsh's 1978 novel, *Grave Mistake*, the gardener is also under suspicion. Ngaio Marsh (1895–1982) was appropriately christened for the purpose of this book. Her first name, pronounced "NYE-oh," is the Maori word for a small, flowering tree. Marsh was born and died in Christchurch, New Zealand.

An artist, interior designer, theatrical director and producer, Marsh gained worldwide recognition through crime fiction that she began to write in her thirties. In the five decades that followed, she completed thirty-two detective novels featuring the poetry-quoting Chief Inspector Roderick Allyn. Although she split her time between New Zealand and

England, Marsh chose to set her mysteries in the latter. Like her fellow queens of crime—Christie, Sayers, and Margery Allingham—Dame Ngaio was awarded the Order of the British Empire.

As the curtain rises on the decidedly horticultural *Grave Mistake*, we find the Kentish garden owners of Upper Quintern in a proper pickle. The sole gardener-for-hire in this village is the irascible and tetchy Angus McBride. His corner on the market ends in two ways: with the appearance of Bruce Gardener, who moves in with his recently widowed sister, and McBride's abrupt, unsuspicious death. (He suffered a massive coronary while readying a client's rose garden for a party.) Bruce Gardener arrives with sterling references—those requisite statements of character and capacity—plus a portfolio of prior projects and an oddly heavy Scottish brogue.

The members of the propertied class quickly hire Gardener-the-gardener and are generally pleased with the results. One of them is Verity Preston, a playwright editing a new script. While Bruce frees her from weeding—and his horticultural competencies in plant selection, soil preparation, and maintenance standards get frequent reference—he still strikes her as too good to be true. Verity, sitting at her desk, simply can't concentrate:

> [She] read the same bit of dialogue three times without reading it at
> all, cast away her pen, swore and went for a walk in her garden. There
> was no doubt that Bruce had done all the right things. There was no
> greenfly on the roses. Hollyhocks and delphiniums flourished against
> the lovely brick wall round her elderly orchard. He had not attempted
> to foist calceolarias upon her or indeed any objectionable annuals: only
> night-scented stocks.

Something about Bruce strikes a dissonant chord, but he isn't the only person in Upper Quintern who seems dodgy.

The village's two main residences are classic settings for this plot and its players. An exquisite Georgian manor house, Quintern Place, has ancient oaks and walled kitchen and rose gardens. It is the property of the Honorable Sybil Foster, now widowed. Its French windows open out to a quintessential English prospect: the rolling Weald of Kent, embracing as its focal point the church of St. Crispin's-in-Quintern. Further down the hill in location and prestige is Mardling Manor, a Victorian extravagance built with turrets and hubris. It may be hideous, but it *is* huge. Its latest occupant is a Greek tycoon with his eye on the house uphill. By coincidence or design, his son is engaged to Sybil Foster's daughter.

Upper Quintern society is small and, like many insular groups, simultaneously amicable and dysfunctional. In some ways, the book is a satire of class. Villagers work as household staff or garden laborers. Outsiders, like Bruce Gardener and Dr. Basil Schramm from the nearby resort spa, rely on introductions to gain admittance to the inner circle of village society. After someone turns up dead, Ngaio Marsh enlists her favorite hero, Detective Inspector Roderick Alleyn of Scotland Yard, to spot the murderer.

THE VEGETABLE GARDENER

Rather than flower gardeners, vegetable growers are added to the suspect list in K. C. Constantine's 1982 mystery, *The Man Who Liked Slow*

Tomatoes. The lead character, Mario Balzic, is a cross between two stereotypes: upright police chief and classic bigot.

Chief Balzic is complicated. He has some bad, if not offensive, attitudes. His language may fit the period, profanity-laced with racial and homophobic slurs. A family-oriented, hard-drinking, hard-boiled, and soft-hearted man, he runs the police department in Rocksburg, a blue-collar coal town in western Pennsylvania already sliding into its post-industrial slump. When ripe tomatoes start showing up in June in town—a solid month ahead of the usual schedule—it signals the start of something strange.

My first garden was in a neighborhood where the gardeners—first-generation children of Italian immigrant parents—demonstrated amazing horticultural skills. Tomato growing was an art, a discipline, and something close to a sacrament. One diminutive gray-haired man planted his seedlings by the phases of the moon. Another swore by starting his seeds indoors on St. Patrick's Day. (The Emerald Isle connection puzzled me until this particular gardener floated the argument that Ireland's shamrock-bishop had been born to Roman parents.) A third visited the local abattoir for buckets of beef blood, his ritual plant food for the tomato patch. Irrespective of method, their results were delicious.

The tomato growers in Constantine's mystery are equally devoted, though Chief Balzic isn't one of them. As the daughter of one of the gardeners explains:

> Planting a garden, my God, there ain't—isn't—nothing more serious than that. He has the priest come and bless the ground. Yeah. He gives the priest a bottle of wine and two dollars. It's the same every year. And the priest comes! And brings holy water and walks all around the garden sprinkling water and praying.

If this resonates, the garden descriptions in Constantine's mystery are worth the wait. They, along with a corpse buried in the garden, appear in the second half of the book. Among the principal suspects are the victim's spouse, various drug-dealing ne'er-do-wells, and one tomato-growing gardener.

THE CACTUS-COLLECTING VICAR AND THE FOUNTAIN ENTHUSIAST

Gardening is not for the faint-hearted, and neither is marriage if you are Lord Peter Wimsey and Harriet Vane. After several novels-worth of uncertainty in their romantic affair, they at last tie the knot in *Busman's Honeymoon*. And what a wedding gift Wimsey has arranged! When he had learned of his fiancée's ambition to possess Talboys, an Elizabethan farmhouse remembered from her Hertfordshire childhood, he bought it from its present owner, Mr. Noakes. All is arranged for them to take possession immediately after the wedding ceremony, or so Lord Peter thinks.

When they arrive at Talboys with Bunter—trusted valet—neither Noakes nor the keys are to be found. They check with the house cleaner, who lives with her son in a cottage on the grounds, to no avail. At last, they track down the front and back door keys when they seek out Miss Twitterton, Noakes's niece in the village.

But once inside, everything is topsy turvy. The house has been emptied of the lovely oak furniture Harriet remembers from house calls with her doctor father. Instead, the rooms are crammed with castoffs and bric-a-brac. There seem to be aspidistras everywhere, and cacti abound in planters and a large hanging pot. A pity the weather is chilly, as the chimneys are blocked and the oil stove smokes. The indoor plumbing is limited.

None of this dampens the spirits or the wedding night of Vane and Wimsey. The next morning dawns bright. Bunter has procured fresh baked goods and the ministrations of a chimney sweep. Harriet steps outside and has a pleasant surprise:

> The garden, at any rate, had been well looked after. There were cabbages at the back, and celery trenches, also an asparagus bed well strawed up and a number of scientifically pruned apple trees. There was also a small cold-house sheltering a hardy vine with half a dozen bunches of black grapes on it and a number of half-hardy plants in pots. In front of the house, a good show of dahlias and chrysanthemums and a bed of scarlet salvias lent color to the sunshine. Mr. Noakes apparently had some little taste for gardening, or at any rate a good gardener; and this was the pleasantest thing yet known of Mr. Noakes, thought Harriet.

The once-a-week gardener, Frank Crutchley, keeps the garden in splendid order. Too bad he becomes a suspect in a murder, when a body—Noakes—is discovered in the cellar. Everyone had disliked Noakes, be they relation, acquaintance, or employee. Noakes had cheated the gardener out of a considerable sum. The niece, Miss Twitterton, had "expectations." A police constable was his blackmail victim. And don't forget the cactus-obsessed vicar who has long envied Noakes's collection. They are all on the suspect list, and the newlyweds are on the case.

In a side plot that has nothing to do with horticultural villainy, Peter and Harriet visit his family seat, Duke's Denver, with notable landscaped grounds. There are terraces opening onto a grand prospect. An orangery and peacocks are present and accounted for. The property boasts a pagoda by Sir William Chambers, who built the Great Pagoda at Kew in 1761 for

Princess Augusta. Unfortunately, the fountains in the water garden are not running that day.

The opposite is the case in "The Fountain Plays," the closing story of Sayers's 1933 anthology, *Hangman's Holiday*. Its plume of water is spraying fifteen feet high, cooling the air with its pleasant spray. Mr. Spiller, the garden's owner, is very much a person of interest. He is also puffed with pride for his new fountain. "I must say I like a bit of ornamental water," he boasts to his dinner guests. "Gives a finish to the place." His future son-in-law calls it "the Versailles touch," with, one thinks, a touch of sarcasm. In just over a dozen pages, the efficient Sayers packs in a discussion of alternative garden designs, blackmail, seduction, and a murder. When the sundry beans are spilled, Sayers reveals whether Spiller is the villain.

THE LEAST LIKELY GARDENER

Hercule Poirot encounters a simpler garden with fewer suspects in the short story "How Does Your Garden Grow?" First published in *Ladies Home Journal* and *The Strand Magazine* in 1935, Agatha Christie included it in a later book-length collection, *The Regatta Mystery and Other Stories*.

The Belgian detective has journeyed to Rosebank, the modest country home of Amelia Barrowsby, a prospective client with whom he has been corresponding. He doesn't expect to meet her. Through his secretary, Miss Lemon, Poirot has learned of Barrowsby's sudden, unexpected death.

Heading toward Rosebank's front door, Poirot is favorably impressed by the almost-symmetrical beds on either side of the walk. They are balanced and tidy, accented with roses pruned into standards and flowering bulbs. The beds are edged, in part, with shells. The design brings to Poirot's mind the nursery rhyme that inquires of Mistress Mary, "How does your garden

grow?" The response of "bluebells and cockle shells" doesn't prevent him from wishing the edging was complete.

A postmortem reveals a fatal dose of strychnine, and Poirot sets out to discover how it was administered. Miss Barrowsby's niece, her nephew by marriage, and the nurse-attendant are all in the picture, though only one of them is a gardener. And there is something about the garden that still nags at Monsieur Poirot... In "How Does Your Garden Grow?" Christie showcased one of her favorite mystery tropes: the least-likely-person motif. In other words, pin the crime on the person who appears entirely innocent.

THE MOST LIKELY GARDENER

G. K. Chesterton used the opposite tactic for his Father Brown mystery, "The Perishing of the Pendragons." In it, Father Brown arrives by yacht with friends to visit Admiral Pendragon at his Elizabethan estate on the Cornish coast. The garden is not much to brag about, with "three circular garden beds, one of red tulips, a second of yellow tulips, and the third of some white, waxen-looking blossoms that the visitors did not know and presumed to be exotic." The man in charge of the garden is even worse, "a heavy, hairy and rather sullen-looking gardener," first encountered "hanging up a heavy coil of garden hose." The gardener indeed turns out to be a rogue, if one in a lineup of rogues. Father Brown's deductions, plus his sudden desire to weed the lawn and his precise aim with the aforesaid garden hose, save the day and the last of the Pendragons.

Sometimes the villain is more engaging than the hero, and gardeners make great suspects. This fact was not lost on the modern-day game designers who came up with *Clue FX*, an electronic revamp of the classic board game that features Rusty, an embittered gardener, and Lord Gray, a cartographer who has turned to garden design in retirement. Dr. Orchid arrived in the latest edition. Her field is plant toxicology.

Having to invent suspects, clues, motive, means, detectives, and more, keeps mystery writers well occupied in the fictional realm. Some balance their literary work with personal forays into horticulture. A garden is a break from the keyboard. The incessant demands of editors, publicists, and readers can, for a time, be set aside for the simple needs of *green growing things*.

MYSTERY WRITERS AND THEIR GARDENS

The Poisoned Pen—and Trowel

For writers of horticultural crime fiction, their expertise with plants fits hand-in-gardening-glove with their prolific pens.

NATHANIEL HAWTHORNE'S LANDSCAPES

Writer's block is nothing new. Once, when addressing his editor, Nathaniel Hawthorne explained his reluctant pen. "An engagement to write must in its nature be conditional; because stories grow like vegetables, and are not manufactured like a pine table." Through his life Hawthorne grew real vegetables and laced his mysterious fiction with garden references.

Even his name has a horticultural ring to it. On reaching the age of majority, Nathaniel Hathorne added a letter to his family name. "Hawthorne" mimics the antique spelling of the common name for a thorny genus grown on both sides of the Atlantic. Born on the Fourth of July 1804, his Puritan roots ran deep into Massachusetts soil. His great-grandfather, John Hathorne, was a judge at the Salem witch trials. Nathaniel Hawthorne's tendency to write about "the evil that men do" likely emerged from that branch of the family.

As to his horticultural bent, many of his Puritan forebears were farmers. His father, a sea captain, died of yellow fever in Surinam when Nathaniel was four years old. Young Nathaniel was raised by his mother and her siblings in Salem, Massachusetts. His uncle Robert Manning—a horticulturist and nurseryman whose *Book of Fruits* (1838) was the standard text on its sweet subject for mid-century Americans—was a key figure in his childhood. His sister Priscilla asked Robert to advise the young boy. "However rich the soil," she wrote in her letter, "we do not expect fruit, unless good seed is sown, and the plants carefully cultivated."

Manning cultivated his nephew's future, creating a microclimate with a steady education: tutors, boarding school, and a large library. Nathaniel was fond of travel books, including the writings of American botanist-explorer William Bartram. His formal education culminated at Bowdoin College in Maine. There he decided that being a minister was "too dull a life" and "as to Lawyers there are so many of them already that one half of them (upon a moderate calculation) are in a state of actual starvation." Being a physician was out of the question since he "should not like to live by the diseases and infirmities of my fellow Creatures." Finally, Hawthorne decided on "becoming an Author and relying for support upon my pen."

He took a winding path to his goal. A publisher in Boston brought out his first book, *Twice-Told Tales*, in 1837. Then he tried a stint working at the

Salem Custom House. In 1841, Hawthorne moved to the fledgling Brook Farm, a utopian experiment on an expansive West Roxbury, Massachusetts, plot of land. There, he hoped to write again and to find a pleasant situation for himself and his betrothed, Sophia Peabody.

He arrived in early spring with snow falling. In the six months from April to October, he worked fields, milked cows, and spread mountains of manure. Early on, he signed his letters "Nathaniel Hawthorne, Ploughman." But he quickly discovered that agricultural labor and intellectual pursuits don't necessarily mix. Writing to Sophia, he moaned, "A man's soul may be buried and perish under a dung-heap or in a furrow of the field, just as well as under a pile of money." In the short months he spent at Brook Farm, Hawthorne did gather much of the material that would appear a decade later as *The Blithedale Romance*. Its poet-protagonist, Miles Coverdale, concludes, "Burns never made a song in haying time. He was no poet while a farmer, and no farmer while a poet." At the end of the story, the exhausted Coverdale packs his bags and departs from his tarnished Arcadia, just as Hawthorne had done.

Eighteen forty-two was a pivotal year. After leaving Brook Farm, Haw-thorne managed to scrape together enough material for a second volume of *Twice-Told Tales*, published the same year. Sales were modest, despite Edgar Allan Poe's thumbs-up review in *Graham's Magazine*. It left Hawthorne unsure about his ability to support himself with his pen, but regardless, he and Sophia wed in Boston that July.

The newlyweds rented the Old Manse in Concord. The property boasted an ancient apple orchard installed by Ralph Waldo Emerson's stepfather, a Unitarian minister. They could hear apples falling "from the mere necessity of perfect ripeness." Everything seemed to be ripening in these honeymoon days. They cultivated their first real garden, a garden plowed and planted by Henry David Thoreau. A daughter, Una, was born, the first of their three children. Emerson and Thoreau were regular visitors.

Nathaniel Hawthorne (1804–1864).

During these three idyllic years in Concord, Hawthorne also had a bountiful professional harvest. His regular output of short stories sold well to periodicals; the mystery "Rappaccini's Daughter" was among them. Later, he published a set called *Mosses from an Old Manse*. This fertile ground also yielded Hawthorne's first and arguably most famous novel, *The Scarlet Letter*, with Hester Prynne wearing her embroidered scarlet "A."

After the publication of *The Scarlet Letter* in 1850, the Hawthornes moved west to the Berkshire Mountains to a small farmhouse "as red as the Scarlet Letter" called Tanglewood. It was on a Lenox, Massachusetts, estate, now the summer venue of the Boston Symphony Orchestra and its famous music festival. Hawthorne "planted vegetables enough to supply all Salem." Sophia planted a flower garden overflowing with tiger lilies, peonies, and columbine.

In Lenox, Hawthorne befriended Herman Melville and began work on *The House of the Seven Gables*. The decaying house at the story's center, with its elm "of wide circumference," holds a curse from the days of the early Puritan settlement. It has a garden, with an ancient rose bush and a congregation of "aristocratic flowers," and "plebian vegetables," despite the "wilderness of neglect." While writing the novel, Hawthorne contrasted his mood with the task at hand:

> The summer is not my natural season for work; and I often find myself gazing at Monument Mountain broad before my eyes, instead of the infernal sheet of paper under my hand. However, I make some little progress ... If not, it can't be helped. I must not pull up my cabbage by the roots, by way of hastening its growth.

Hawthorne managed to finish *Seven Gables* that year. But his wanderlust resurfaced. And so the Hawthornes moved again, back to Concord where they bought property for the first time. The Wayside was the former home of the Alcotts and around the corner from the Emersons.

It turned out to be a temporary wayside, since the next year his friend and fellow Bowdoin alumnus, Franklin Pierce, was elected President of the United States. He appointed Hawthorne US Consul to England. Off the Hawthornes went, bag and baggage, to Liverpool. In addition to his duties, Hawthorne enjoyed excursions to English gardens such as Blenheim. But for the next four years his literary output was almost nil. Evidently the diplomatic service sapped his pen as much as farm labor. After his term as consul expired, Hawthorne chose the route of many mid-century authors and artists and transferred his household to Italy.

In Florence, the Hawthornes occupied the ground floor suite in the Casa del Bello. It had a garden, "a little wilderness of shrubbery and roses," Sophia wrote, with a terrace and summerhouse where her husband could sit "dreaming of a story." His study overlooked the garden; perhaps it summoned the memory of his earlier protagonist, Giovanni, who had looked out over Signor Rappaccini's poisonous plants. The next year, when they lived in Rome, under the influence of its old villa gardens, Hawthorne conceived of his final novel, *The Marble Faun*. In its introduction, he notes, "Romance and poetry, ivy, lichens, and wall-flowers, need ruin to make them grow."

There is a murder in *The Marble Faun* (1859), but it is more gothic than crime fiction. Its characters stroll through many famous Italian sites, including the gardens of the Villa Medici. Hawthorne's descriptions of its hedges, fountains, and flower beds makes him one of the first Americans to write about gardens of the Renaissance style, well before Edith Wharton's *Italian Villas and their Gardens*, first printed as a series of articles in *The Century* in 1903. This places Hawthorne's novel at the leading edge of a passion for the Italianate in American gardens.

From Italy, Hawthorne moved first to England, and then back to Concord, rounding out the travelogue that is his biography. In his final collection, *Our Old House*, Hawthorne, who has always struck me as vaguely archaic, sounds like a contemporary ecologist. "Perhaps if we could penetrate Nature's secrets we should find that what we call weeds are more essential to the well-being of the world, than the most precious fruit or grain."

AGATHA CHRISTIE'S GARDENS

Agatha Mary Clarissa Miller was a surprise, starting with a mother and father who had assumed their childbearing phase was done. Her brother Monty and her sister Madge were older by a decade or more and already well into their school years when she appeared. A cherished late arrival, Agatha had a happy upbringing, surrounded by adults and her teenaged siblings. At the end of her life, her memories glowed with loving parents, a devoted nanny, and a country house, Ashfield, in Torquay on the south coast of Devon. It was more villa than mansion, a comfortable homey place. Her most vivid recollections were of its magical garden.

"The garden was to mean more and more to me, year after year," she wrote in her autobiography. Not the kitchen garden which, other than providing opportunities to purloin ripe fruit, was something of a bore. It was the garden proper with its lawn studded with specimen trees that caught her fancy, a jewel box arboretum planted by some earlier owner.

There were textured evergreens: broadleaf ilex, needled cedar, and two firs that had been claimed by siblings Monty and Madge. Her sister's tree had a curved branch that formed a comfortable seat, a safe and surreptitious hideaway. A display of arboreal curiosities included an "excitingly tall" Wellingtonia—better known in America as California redwood, a Chilean monkey puzzle tree, spiky and reptilian, and one she called the turpentine

tree, though whether a pine, eucalyptus, or other exotic is open to spec-
ulation. Agatha's best-loved was the great beech, its spreading limbs and
elephant skin trunk enhanced by a steady supply of beechnuts in season.

Beyond the garden were the woods, principally ash, as "Ashfield"
implies. They loomed largest in her childhood world, a place of mystery,
intrigue, and forbidden things. Their zigzagging path was a road to adventure, perfumed with innocence. She populated her universe with imaginary
playmates, starting with an invisible litter of kittens.

She remembered Ashfield for autumn and winter, those seasons of trees,
and her grandmother's garden in Ealing, West London, for summer and roses.
(That grandmother, Margaret Miller, was both her mother's aunt and her
father's stepmother.) The Ealing rose garden wasn't large but was an object
of pride. It was deadheaded daily and fed, as her grandmother boasted, with
"the bedroom slops, my dear. Liquid manure–nothing like it!" I feel certain
that "Auntie-Grannie" and her circle of courteous, clever, and exacting friends
contributed traits to the future personality of Christie's Miss Jane Marple.

Agatha's father, Frederick Miller, died when she was eleven. The last years
of his life had been plagued by financial worries; the fortune accumulated by
his American father, in the form of a trust fund, seems to have been misman-
aged by its trustees. As a widow, her mother economized and considered
selling Ashfield. The protests from her three children were so vehement,
she abandoned the idea. Her daughter Madge, now married, later joined
by Agatha, contributed toward its upkeep. Around this time Madge bet
Agatha that she couldn't write a detective story, something along the lines
of their favorite selections from *The Adventures of Sherlock Holmes*.

In 1913, just before the outbreak of war, Agatha met Archie Christie, a
junior Army officer in training as a pilot in the new Royal Flying Corps.
They married eighteen months later, during one of his leaves. While he
fought in France, she worked as an unpaid nurse and, after passing quali-
fying exams, a paid pharmacy assistant at a Red Cross hospital operating

in Torquay's converted town hall. In her free time, she wrote what would become *The Mysterious Affair at Styles*.

Archie returned in 1918. They rented a flat in London; the next year, their daughter Rosalind was born. The Bodley Head, a London publishing house, brought out Agatha's first book in 1920, and she signed a contract for four more. Feeling flush with Agatha's earnings, the Christies bought an elegant home in Sunningdale, some thirty miles from the center of London. They called their property "Styles," in honor of her novel. The house and gardens were lovely, though Agatha was too busy with writing and child-rearing to enjoy them. It was a stressful time. The Christies' relationship became more and more strained.

By 1926, things fell apart. After her mother died that April, Agatha floated for months in a limbo of depression. Archie, by this time in love with another woman, asked for a divorce in August. Agatha Christie, with full custody of Rosalind, continued to use her first married name as a professional pen name, even after her second marriage to archaeologist Max Mallowan in 1930. During a long and happy life with Max, she found time to return to a garden.

But not at Ashfield. Mass tourism had discovered Torquay. The adjacent neighborhood had built up, ruining Ashfield's views with a pileup of holiday homes and institutions. Her "*chère maison*" had turned into "a parody of itself." With regret, she sold it in 1940; it has since been demolished. In 1946, she wrote *The Hollow*, a Hercule Poirot mystery with a vivid description of the landscape at "Ainswick," the childhood home of two of its main characters. Her detailed portrayal of the gardens recalls Ashfield, down to the giant beech, the Wellingtonia, and the meandering path through a magical wood.

Fortunately for Christie, the loss of Ashfield was buffered by a new acquisition. By chance, Agatha and Max had found a house on the market that she had known during her youth. Greenway, about ten miles from Torquay, was built on a promontory that sweeps down to the River Dart. Its gleaming white Georgian house, though marred by later additions, had

Agatha Christie (1890–1976) and her many titles.

Agatha Christie and Max Mallowan at their beloved Greenway.

unsullied views of river and wooded hills. "Why don't you buy it?" said Max. So, in 1938, she did, for a holiday getaway to complement a London flat and Winterbrook, their Oxfordshire home.

They pulled down Greenway's additions and updated the original structure with modern conveniences. Outdoors, they began to uncover the rare plants in its overgrown gardens. There was an admirable collection of rhododendrons, camellias, and specimen trees, acquired by a century of Greenway's earlier owners from famous nurseries like Veitch and Caerhays. She and Max—now Professor Sir Max Mallowan—began to add plantings of their own. He referred to them as "our children, yours and mine." These were noteworthy children, including many specimen camellias.

It was at Greenway that she learned, for the second time in her life, that Britain was at war with Germany. The Admiralty requisitioned Greenway in 1942 for the duration of the hostilities. Officers of the United States Navy occupied the house for six months. Max served in the Royal Air Force, and Agatha stayed in London, as did Rosalind who was now married with a child of her own. At the end of 1945, the Mallowans reclaimed their holiday home, in reasonably good condition save the dozen or so lavatories installed near the kitchen. They restored the gardens, grown into "a beautiful jungle," with the help of a competent but dictatorial head gardener, Mr. Lavin, whom Christie nicknamed "Hitler-Lavin." They delighted in the house and gardens for the rest of their lives.

Agatha Christie died in 1976 at Winterbrook. She was buried in the churchyard at St. Mary's Church in nearby Cholsey. An ancient yew cast its shade on the graves at the time, though it was felled by a heavy storm in 1989.

Early on, Christie had made Greenway the setting for new mysteries, including *Five Little Pigs*, originally published in 1942 as *Murder in Retrospect*. In it, Poirot deduces the truth about a murder that happened years before in a Devon garden overlooking the river—renamed the Helm. *Dead Man's Folly*, published in 1956, has scenes in a thinly disguised Greenway boathouse. For fans of David Suchet's portrayal of Poirot, one of his last appearances in the ITV series *Dead Man's Folly*, was filmed on location at Greenway in 2013 with its rhododendrons in full bloom.

Though Christie died almost half a century ago, her cunning tales of murder and detection still fill bookstore mystery sections and inspire adaptations and spinoffs in film, broadcast, and other media. Her daughter and grandson gifted Greenway to the National Trust in 2000. The gardens opened soon afterward, followed by the renovated house in 2009. New generations of fans are invited to explore the property, recognized as a "Garden of Excellence" by the International Camellia Society. Agatha Christie called it "the loveliest place in the world."

REX STOUT'S PLANTS

In addition to crafting Nero Wolfe mysteries, Rex Stout was an indoor plant whiz. At least as interesting as his protagonist, Stout had also been, at various times, a childhood math prodigy, a sailor on Theodore Roosevelt's presidential yacht, a farmer, the head of the War Writers' Board, and a radio host.

Watering his collection of houseplants—approximately three hundred of them—was a meditative task. Ideas for plots often coalesced while he was thus engaged. But once he sat down to write, he delegated the horticultural chores to his agreeable spouse. She was his houseplant sidekick, the Theodore Horstmann to his Nero Wolfe. Unlike Wolfe, orchids were not among Stout's favorite plants.

Rex Stout the gardener did not limit himself to indoor plants. He filled the ample grounds that surrounded High Meadow, his house near Danbury, Connecticut, with vegetables and fruits, trees and flowering

Rex Stout (1886–1975).

shrubs, and perennials like daylilies. It was the iris that stole his heart. On his 80th birthday, the Associated Press reported that he grew 192 varieties of tall, bearded irises. He called one of his iris beds—measuring three feet by thirty—"Rhapsody in Blue." There he planted a study in color, a progression of blue cultivars from the pale 'Azure Skies' through the velvet darkness of 'Black Hills'.

His sister Ruth Stout was a successful garden writer, known best for her principles of "No-Work" gardening. (*The*

Washington Post called her "The Mother of Mulch.") She gave her younger brother Rex the third degree in an interview with him for the June 1956 issue of *Popular Gardening*. In true sibling fashion, he started off by goading her. Irises do not like mulch. "And *you* turning yourself inside out trying to coax everybody to mulch everything all year round," he taunted. "Are you sure you're broadminded enough to write about an exception?"

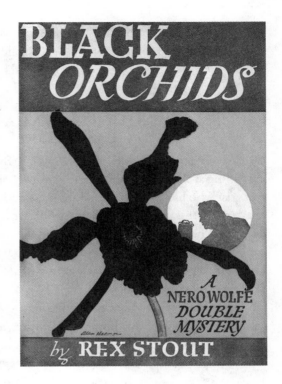

By then aged 70, Rex Stout had been growing irises for a quarter century. In the interview, he described his meticulous methods, including record keeping. In a black loose-leaf binder, Stout kept a page on each of his nearly two hundred iris varieties. At bloom time he presided as judge, issuing a "V" for "Verdict" to every variety. "V-F" was "Verdict-Fair," "V-G" for "Verdict-Good," "V-E" for "Verdict-Excellent" and so on, up to "V-W." Trouble was, there were too many rated "Verdict-Wonderful."

His writing process was just as disciplined. "I write for 39 consecutive days each year," he once explained. Taking out time for weekends and holidays, "I figure on six weeks for a book, but I shave it down." Rex Stout's discipline paid off. He masterminded forty-six Nero Wolfe mysteries between the early thirties—*Fer-de-Lance* appeared in 1934—and his death in 1975 at age 88.

KAREN HUGG'S BALANCING ACT

Garden writers share a common complaint. They spend too much time gardening at the keyboard. Karen Hugg (pronounced "hewg"), a horticulturist who has written four murder mysteries and a wellness book, has tried to foil this dilemma by drafting her latest manuscript outdoors. But a laptop is neither a soil knife nor a pair of pruners. "To write," Hugg explains on a recent August day, "I have to be sedentary and focused on an imaginary world," a world that unfortunately must take shape on a computer monitor.

The word *write* could be an antonym for *garden*. To tend a garden is active, a physical cadence of weeding, transplanting, and trimming. Try as one might to ignore them, the plants are calling.

Karen Hugg.

A better strategy for Hugg has been seasonal, writing during the wet, colder months of her Pacific Northwest winters, then turning her attention to the garden with the lengthening days. She engages in active horticulture not just for herself but also for clients. If Hugg's schedule of writing, maintaining her garden, and running a business seems onerous, it makes more sense given her personal history.

After graduate school, she was an editor, first for small publishing houses and then in high tech. Employers like Amazon and Microsoft had monetary advantages but a grueling pace. After corporate burn-out, these jobs left her with endurance for long work weeks that served Hugg well on her next path.

Her love affair with plants started with a single shrub. It was a butterfly bush, *Buddleia davidii* 'Black Knight'. Blame a nursery catalog and its come-hither description of the plant as a butterfly magnet. It didn't seem possible. Skepticism aside, Hugg succumbed, buying a 'Black Knight' for what she calls her "shabby little yard." Magic happened; the butterflies arrived. "Ha, I was so naïve then," she recalls with a laugh. One plant led to another and another, and eventually led her to horticulture school and a fresh start as a professional gardener.

That single butterfly bush is now surrounded by an abundance of ornamentals on a new property, full of designed spaces. A grove of native conifers, underplanted with ferns, leads up to the traditional, colonial-style house. In the back, a deep stretch of lawn is surrounded by curving borders. A romp of sun-loving perennials and woody plants—hebe, ceanothus, lilac, magnolia, mock orange, and viburnum—fills a bed nicknamed "California" for its dry situation. If, like me, you live in cooler climes, you may have a tinge of zone envy from her description of her "Hawaii" border, lush with loquat, fig, and the fireworks of Chilean fire bush—there's a reason why Seattle has been called gardening heaven. But gardeners everywhere will take comfort from Hugg's reaction to the overgrown shrubs along the front of her house. "It's messy, so cover your eyes." That project hasn't made it to the top of the priority list. Yet.

For a long time, Karen Hugg the writer barred plants from her fiction. Her garden was soul-soothing, her own private sanctum. It seemed to have no place in mysteries. Until it did. Inspiration comes unbidden from various quarters, including the horticultural realm.

As Hugg notes, "Plants are amazing because they're both charmingly delicate and incredibly resilient. They're also brimming with beauty and sex." The survival strategies and defenses of the plant kingdom—their thorns, poisons, and alluring scents—struck home. "What would happen if a flower emitted a dangerous scent to inhale," she pondered. "How would that work?" That question morphed into *The Forgetting Flower*.

Unlike gardening, discovered in her twenties, Hugg has always loved to read. Her father died when she was a child, and the world of books provided temporary distraction, a place where imagined adventure and romance ousted sadness. She got hooked on mysteries as an adult reader.

The no-nonsense prose of early detective fiction—writers like Dashiell Hammett, Agatha Christie, Walter Mosley, and Dorothy L. Sayers—has special appeal for Hugg. Tana French is her model of a modern fiction stylist for the "tight energy" in her novels. She adds Ruth Ware, Elizabeth George, Donna Leon, and Attica Locke to her list of favorites, citing their frameworks, their textures of custom, culture, and setting.

Hugg's detailed knowledge of Paris for *The Forgetting Flower* came from her time living there as part of the launch team for *amazon.fr*. Negotiating the city's fashionable quarters and more complex neighborhoods in her too-rare downtime, she noticed parks, gardens, and flower boxes. The plants were both exotic and familiar, as growing conditions in Paris match Seattle's. Best of all were the tiny flower shops, "little oases of green in a concrete city." They became prototypes for the bijou boutique managed by her novel's protagonist.

Several villains lurk in the story line of *The Forgetting Flower*. Some of them hide out in her garden beds. Top of her botanical most-wanted list is the morning glory. "Just when I think I've pulled every root, it comes back to haunt me," she groans. English ivy is a close second.

If one broadens the definition to include animals, her major adversary is the mole. It is the Moriarity to her Sherlock. Moles seem to target the root zones of her rarest, most expensive plant acquisitions for their tunnels. Perhaps they are one reason her current project is nonfiction: how to relieve stress through gardening.

VICKI LANE'S FARM

In the raised beds, dark green parsley, golden oregano, and purple-leafed sage crowded one another, while the bright chartreuse and deep burgundy of loose-leaf lettuces scrolled in bold patterns. Elizabeth had discovered long ago that dividing each rectangular bed into three triangles and then planting contrasting colors and textures within each division would produce a kind of cut-rate formal garden—at least till all the lettuce was harvested.

FROM *SIGNS IN THE BLOOD*, BY VICKI LANE

Vicki Lane loves gardening. She came by it naturally, with grandparents and parents who took pains with plantings around their homes. Growing up, a typical destination for a Sunday drive was a nursery. Thus, the happy process of choosing, transplanting, tending, and watching plants grow was passed on in the normal course of things. She shares a favorite childhood book with many gardeners—*The Secret Garden* by Frances Hodgson Burnett—along with the nature writing of Gene Stratton-Porter.

When Lane got her own bit of earth, she had a big canvas to work with. In the nineteen-seventies, Vicki and her husband John moved from Tampa's suburbs to one hundred acres in rural North Carolina. Their farm is nestled in the Great Smokies, a rolling mountainscape at the southern edge of the Appalachians not far from the Tennessee border. Much of the property is wooded, though there was plenty of space for cash crops, a large, terraced vegetable garden, and what would, over time, become her version of an English cottage garden. The labor was all their own.

Mystery writing came a quarter century later. She was, in a sense, picking up the thread of an earlier career. (Lane has a master's degree in English Literature and taught at a prep school.) By the time she sat down to write her first novel, her two children were grown, the garden well established, if demanding. "Gardening was the basis, the backbone, of what I did," she explained.

Daylight hours were spent working in the garden. Then, from 9:00 p.m. until midnight, she would write, fingers on keyboard, illuminated by the computer screen. The following day she could often resolve sticky plot points during the meditative round of gardening tasks, and commit them to the page later that night.

Open any of her six Elizabeth Goodweather mysteries, and you will feel right at home. The reason is simple, Lane says. "When I wrote about Elizabeth, her house is very much our house, where I live. I made it easy on myself by writing about what I saw every day, what I had seen for years and years." You'll want to join Elizabeth on her comfortable front porch. Sit and visit for a spell. Take in the view. Or perhaps you'd like to see the garden.

Vicki Lane.

It is natural that Elizabeth's tiered vegetable garden mimics her creator's. With southern exposure and perfect drainage, Lane's raised beds yielded bumper crops season after season, despite battles with blight and blossom-eating deer. For many years running, a hundred quart jars of

Vicki Lane's North Carolina garden.

home-grown, home-canned tomatoes glistened from the pantry shelves by the end of harvest. When Lane wrote *Art's Blood*, one fan from Hawaii told her that the page-long, mouthwatering description of Elizabeth's tomatoes should be labeled as tomato porn. It is a sensory feast converted to print. Reading her books can increase one's appetite.

Her Goodweather mysteries are also a love song to her garden. The garden descriptions sing from the page, and she takes care in writing about plants. A journal that she had kept for many years, with its record of weather and the day-to-day timing of garden and forest, was a help along the way. "When I teach writing, I tell people to make sure they are accurate for the flora of a place. If you're writing about North Carolina mountains, be sure you don't have someone go out under Grandpap's redwood tree."

Lane's painting teacher has called her a colorist, and her skills with color permeate both prose and planting design. "Your garden can be an artistic outlet as well," she suggests. "I enjoy messing around with color." Next to a *Salvia farinacea* 'Victoria Blue', she would seek out something yellow "to make it pop." She plants varieties of lettuce in rectangular boxed beds, laying out designs that show up in Elizabeth's potager in *Signs in the Blood*. If the plantings seem like a quilt block, that reflects Lane's interest in quilting. If they seem like a color-rich potager, it is because she draws inspiration from both French and English garden history.

Local color infuses her writing. Her characters—their personalities, dialect, and culture—evoke nostalgia in many readers, surfacing memories of southern relations. Action plays out in the scenic landscape of hills and hollows, forest and farm. "My Goodweather books are, in a way, a love song to Madison County."

But to call Lane a regional mystery writer seems like calling Emily Dickinson a regional poet because she wrote about the world in and about her Massachusetts home. While Lane's fiction is set in the North Carolina mountains, it deals with themes that apply to us all: portraits of people and place, changes to life and landscape. Another of those themes is aging.

Now when she looks at her garden, she appreciates it with the eye of experience. It has matured under her care. It began with plant offerings from family and friends. Irises and daylilies arrived as donations; she carried on the tradition, sharing divisions in turn. A cutting of mock orange thrived and is well loved, if rambunctious. Great hedges of weigela and forsythia arrived mail order from catalogs, rooted sticks in boxes that were planted with a prayer. A penchant for peonies, especially tree peonies, resulted in a collection that blooms without fail each spring. Dwarf evergreens have become giants.

Her garden is dominated by plants nurtured over five decades. Physically, it is less accessible to her today. As with Christie's Miss Marple, age and an accident have curtailed her hands-on horticulture. Her appreciation persists. Vicki Lane continues to revel in peonies that are "just magical," the elegance of Siberian and Japanese irises, the beauties and mysteries of a garden, sunrise to sunset, every day, in every season.

CYNTHIA RIGGS'S ISLAND

Close to a thousand miles separate Vicki Lane's mountain garden from the West Tisbury, Massachusetts, home of Cynthia Riggs. Riggs lives, writes, and gardens on Martha's Vineyard, an island in the Atlantic off the coast of Cape Cod.

My first encounter with the mysteries of Cynthia Riggs came in audio-book form. The reader was British. Interesting, I thought, as the Yankee dialect of Martha's Vineyard carries traces of its forebears across the sea. When the narrator read the word "compost" as "com-pahst," it set me to wondering. Do Vineyarders pronounce compost with a short "o" like the Brits?

No, Riggs assures me. When she carries garden or kitchen refuse to one of her seven heaps—each bounded by repurposed wooden pallets in good New England fashion—she calls it compost with "a long 'o' as in Poe." One can recognize a true gardener in Riggs's praise of compost. The "very best thing" is to "turn over that rich, black, fluffy stuff that started out as weeds, orange peels, coffee grounds, more weeds." Her protagonist also knows her way around a compost pile.

Lest we think the character of Victoria Trumbull in the series beginning with *Deadly Nightshade* is a self-portrait, Riggs emphasizes that "every single facet of Victoria is my mother." Her mother seemed to know every wild plant on the island, and so does Victoria. If Victoria makes much of her emerging snowdrops, you would be correct in assuming Riggs's mother was an enthusiastic gardener. To give fair credit, so was her father.

In the books, Victoria Trumbull is 92 years old; she does not age—the prerogative of the fiction writer. Dionis Coffin Riggs was 99 at her death in 1997. Dionis was a poet, and "she could have done the Victoria deeds easily." Riggs chose to make VT—as she calls her protagonist—younger simply because a 99-year-old sleuth seemed improbable. "But then, my mother was improbable," she adds.

Perhaps all Riggs women are improbable, or perhaps the island infuses its own brand of energy. (Cynthia is a thirteenth-generation Vineyarder.) In 2000, she earned her MFA in creative writing from Vermont College. It had been forty-seven years—and five children—since her college graduation. In between, she had written for National Geographic, run the Chesapeake Bay Ferry Boat Company, taught at the Annapolis Sailing School, and worked as a rigger in the Martha's Vineyard Shipyard. Should you need a captain for your charter boat, Cynthia has her US Coast Guard 100-ton license.

When Riggs set sail on her career in fiction, she was within hailing distance of her seventieth birthday. A friend suggested she write mysteries. Most of us would be happy to produce one book; Cynthia planned for twenty. The Vineyard was her setting, her mother the detective, and plants served as titles and plot devices. "Characters, since I'm no good at making them up, are all based on real Islanders," she notes. "The Sunday New York Times said my characters don't seem evil, more like 'seriously naughty.'" With her latest book, *Widow's Wreath*, she has reached number fourteen of the twenty.

If her life seems like a wild ride, so is her garden, an abundant mix of invited guests and native plants akin to the Island's human population in season. "My whole place is a tangle of all kinds of growing things, many that simply decided they like to grow here." Her garden romps around Cleaveland House, which has been in her family for more than two and a half centuries.

In 1988, Riggs and her mother began to invite paying guests into three of their second-floor rooms for bed-and-breakfast accommodations. They come in through the back door of the gray house which—"typical New England," as Cynthia explains—they use as the main entrance. To the right is an exuberant patch of flowers. "I've tried to plant a nice tidy entry garden, but the wildflowers won't have it." With black-eyed Susans, goldenrod, asters, and Queen Anne's lace, the bees and butterflies approve.

Cynthia Riggs.

The long borders along the drive that start the growing season with daffodils are filled with milkweed by summer's dog days. A bank of ancient lilacs embraces the house, purple and fragrant against the weathered gray shingles each spring. It vies with the "purple waterfall" of wisteria that her father planted, its trunk now a foot in diameter. There is a brick-bordered herb garden with blackberries, parsley, rue, and arugula. Bee balm grows there, and it made a prominent appearance in *The Bee Balm Murders*:

> The bee balm, in full ragged bloom in Victoria Trumbull's garden, was taller than she'd ever seen it, probably because of the heavy June rains. Victoria, at ninety-two, had known seasons when the minty-smelling plants never bloomed. This year they formed a dense fire-engine-red blanket that she could see from the west window. True to its name, the bee balm resonated with the buzz of honeybees, dozens and dozens in this patch of brilliance.

She reaps what she sows in many ways.

Her substantial vegetable garden, 35-foot square, is filled with tomatoes, kale, chard, collards, and onions. The west fence is covered with hops; its harvest is a principal ingredient in the custom brew at Offshore Ale Pub in Oak Bluffs. On the north side, a kiwi vine took over. Determined, she cut it to two-foot stumps before it sprouted this spring. "Wouldn't you know?" she laughs, instead of taming the plant, the crewcut increased its vigor. As with many writers' gardens, there are plenty of weeds, owing to long hours at the keyboard. Riggs has experimented with an eat-the-weeds method of control for those that are edible, but to her "they just taste green."

She has tried any number of attractive flowers to hide the fill pipe for the underground propane tank, but the chickens and wild turkeys have ravaged them all. When she threw in some pumpkin seeds, the feathered denizens of the property ignored them. Seven pumpkins ripened in this impromptu patch.

She accepts the foibles of her much-loved garden and doesn't remember a time when she didn't love gardening. Now that she is a writer, it pays her back with a new dividend. "What better way to handle a stuck paragraph than to get up from my seat and dig, weed, rake, and just breathe in the wonder of plant life?"

NAOMI HIRAHARA'S GARDENS IN THE JAPANESE STYLE

Sometimes gardening skips a generation. My parents, who grew up shackled by incessant summer weeding of farm and garden, were satisfied as adults to have minimal involvement with plants. Dad mowed the lawn of our suburban corner lot. Mom harvested two perennial crops—chives and mint—from a bed along the back fence and kept a few potted cacti on life support. That was that. Their offspring, throwbacks to gardening grandparents, re-engaged with horticulture. Naomi Hirahara doesn't garden herself, despite her mother's love of gardening and her father's landscape business in Los Angeles. The green thumbprint of her genetics emerged through her writing.

Naomi Hirahara.

In addition to her seven award-winning Mas Arai mysteries, Hirahara has, among her many credits, several nonfiction books on plant-related topics. There is a biography of a Japanese strawberry farmer. *A Scent of Flowers* is a history of the Southern California Flower Market. She edited *Green Makers: Japanese American Gardeners in Southern California* and has curated a number of museum exhibitions. In a 2018 profile, the *Los Angeles Times* called her a "one-woman Japanese American history machine." If you are a film noir fan, look for the short feature, *Mamo's Weeds*, produced by the Japanese American National Museum. Hirahara created both concept and screenplay.

She was weaned on the family landscaping business and its daily rituals of preparation: make lunch, pack the coolers, load the equipment into the truck, watch her father—and later, her younger brother—dress and drive away for all-day horticultural labor in the Los Angeles heat.

It wasn't an easy life. Like her protagonist Mas Arai, her father was born in California and sent to Japan as a young child for the equivalent of grammar and high school. He, and the girl he would later marry, survived the atomic bomb dropped on Hiroshima in 1945, despite their terrifying proximity to the epicenter of the blast.

Isamu "Sam" Hirahara returned to California to a life of hard work. He cut lawns, trimmed shrubs, watered and weeded other people's gardens.

Most of his clients were white, on occasion Tinsel Town celebrities. (Actor Robert Reed, best known as Mike Brady in the seventies sitcom *The Brady Bunch*, was one of them.). As a licensed contractor, Sam Hirahara also built "Oriental" landscapes from scratch.

Naomi joined her father only once on his route. "I did a horrendous job," she remembers, laughing. It was a failed attempt to rake dried sycamore leaves. "I was never invited back!" Nonetheless, his work left its mark on her. The children of Japanese American maintenance gardeners were infused with strong principles: diligence, thoroughness, humility. Her father died in 2012.

These days, seeing a gardener's truck traveling down one of the LA freeways elicits in Hirahara an emotional response. Her books have provided an outlet. "Writing about Mas and his friends is my attempt to immortalize this generation of gardeners, at least on paper."

Beyond personal experience, historic research provides the "fodder," as she calls it, for her mysteries. She depicts culture and community in precise detail, propelling her narratives with accuracy. The Japanese-style garden in America is her fascination, and many appear in her books. How a Japanese-style garden on the east coast—a major public garden at that—became a key setting for *Gasa-Gasa Girl* is best told in Hirahara's own words:

> I told my series editor at the time that I was planning to set my second mystery in New York City because I had happened to place [Arai's daughter] there in my first novel, *Summer of the Big Bachi*. The first book was heavy—there are flashbacks to the Hiroshima bombing—so I wanted to write a more intimate, upstairs-downstairs type of book involving a strained father-daughter relationship. She told me that there was a large Japanese-style garden at the Brooklyn Botanic Garden—thus starting my going down that rabbit hole. It was certainly serendipitous!

I stayed at a bed-and-breakfast in a brownstone in Prospect Park, walking distance from the Botanic Garden. I found a piece of original writing by Takeo Shiota [who had designed the Japanese Hill-and-Pond Garden at the Brooklyn Botanic Garden] at the New York Public Library and was able to get a fuller picture of who he was.

During the Second World War, Japanese Americans like Shiota were incarcerated in one of ten government camps. Even there, in incarceration centers with crowded, tarpaper barracks guarded by soldiers in machine-gun towers, they gardened. Hirahara, who has written on the internment, recounts, "Inmates ordered plants from their friends on the outside and started to create gardens on the inside." One of the men who organized a camp garden "didn't want children in camp to be isolated from the beauty of nature." In the collection of the Library of Congress is a 1943 photograph by Ansel Adams of a manicured hill-and-pond-style garden that inmates built in the high desert of the Manzanar, California camp. At its peak, over 10,000 people were held there, from infant to elder. And still, they gardened. Proof, if proof were needed, that gardens have restorative power.

When she was writing *Green Makers*, Hirahara began to document smaller gardens that Japanese Americans had built for their Southern California communities in the first half of the twentieth century, gestures of friendship on behalf of themselves or their children. During World War II, with its high tide of anti-Japanese sentiment, many of the gardens were covered over or destroyed. Today, decades later, Hirahara finds school students and volunteer groups reclaiming them. "Such a beautiful symbol of reconciliation," she says. Reconciliation and resilience.

Pick a location around the globe and you will likely find a Japanese-style garden. "Its appeal is that it is a world unto itself and, with its twists and turns, the visitor has a unique and sometimes healing experience," explains Hirahara. She has featured many of them in her books: the 1960s garden at Dodger Stadium in *Sayonara Slam*, for instance, or the restored garden in *Hiroshima Boy*. She tried to make the Mas Arai books like those gardens—"I seek to surprise but, in the end, to heal and restore."

Writing murder mysteries is a bit like working in the garden: they start with tangled chaos and end, at least for a moment, in an ordered universe. And while the butler may have done it, I'm happy to say that, at least in fiction, the gardener rarely has.

THE END

Why Gardening Can Be Murder

At the end of a murder mystery, the neatly wrapped solution is unveiled. Horticultural themes have held an outsized place in the genre since Wilkie Collins published his rose-bedecked *The Moonstone* in 1868. It is still going strong. Why?

In gardens, the struggle between life and death is laid bare. Animals eat plants. Pests infest plants. As every experienced gardener knows, gardeners kill plants. Sometimes, as with weeds, these are murders with intent, but often the deaths are accidental. I have a three-strike rule in my garden. If I kill a desired plant three times, that's not the plant for me. Even if justice does not prevail in the garden, horticulture is a perfect fit for crime fiction.

Writers write what they know, and there are many writer-gardeners. In their gardens, or gardens they research, they discover setting, motive, means,

and clue. Gardening offers occupations or avocations for their detectives, suspects, and criminals. The skill of the author transforms the horticultural into the mysterious.

Readers read what appeals. There are many ardent plant lovers among mystery consumers. If, as Margaret Atwood wrote, gardening is not a rational act, gardeners are irrational beings. Last Saturday morning was the annual spring plant sale at the small historic garden where I volunteer. Customers lined up before the 9:00 a.m. opening, despite the cold soaking rain. There they waited with dripping boxes and damp wallets to buy the plants we had potted and priced. And we stood there in the downpour, selling plants and collecting money for our garden. It would have been a perfect day for murder. And it was the perfect day for getting home, running a hot bath, and picking up a good mystery.

BOOK LIST

When I asked Ruth Ware about her inspiration for *The Turn of the Key*, she observed, "Pretty much half the plants in the average cottage garden are toxic to some degree—but we don't think of them as deadly poisons; to us they're just pretty foxgloves or majestic yew trees or cheerful laurels." As case in point, she cited the "humble daffodil" with enough toxicity to bring on acute vomiting if its early leaves are mistaken for green onions. "This reminder of the dangers we take for granted is deliciously fertile ground for a crime writer."

Plants, gardens, and their ties to the mystery genre have also provided fertile ground for me. I share this list of the titles referenced to make it easier for you to track them down. For older, out-of-print books, you may find them on the secondhand market or as ebooks. Sometimes, as with Sheila Pim's *Common or Garden Crime*, a new publisher has reissued them. Check your library's catalog, too; I'm amazed at what the librarians can dig up through our public library consortium.

Crime fiction flourishes these days. The mystery section in my local library has grown from the small bookshelf of my youth to occupy a room of its own. Recommendations are welcome. If you have suggestions for other horticultural mysteries, please drop me a line. You will find an email link on my website: www.martamcdowell.com.

AUTHOR	TITLE	PUBLISHER	FIRST PUBLISHED
Aird, Catherine	*Passing Strange*	Doubleday	1981
Albert, Susan Wittig*	*The Darling Dahlias and the Cucumber Tree*	Berkeley Prime Crime	2010
	Queen Anne's Lace	Berkeley Prime Crime	2018
	Rosemary Remembered	Berkeley Prime Crime	1995
	Rueful Death	Berkeley Prime Crime	1996
Ashley, Jennifer	*Death in Kew Gardens*	Berkeley Prime Crime	2019
Atherton, Nancy	*Aunt Dimity and the Duke*	Viking	1994
Barron, Stephanie	*The White Garden*	Bantam Books	2009
Beaton, M. C.	*Agatha Raisin and the Potted Gardener*	St. Martin's Press	1994
Bradley, Alan*	*The Sweetness at the Bottom of the Pie*	Random House	2009
	The Weed that Strings the Hangman's Bag	Random House	2010
Brown, Rita Mae	*Furmidable Foes*	Bantam Books	2020
Cannon, Taffy	*Tangled Roots*	Carroll & Graf	1995
Chandler, Raymond	*The Big Sleep*	Alfred A. Knopf	1939
Christie, Agatha	*4:50 From Paddington*	Collins Crime Club	1957
	A Caribbean Mystery	Collins Crime Club	1964
	By the Pricking of My Thumbs	Collins Crime Club	1968
	Dead Man's Folly	Collins Crime Club	1956
	Five Little Pigs	Dodd, Mead	1942

AUTHOR	TITLE	PUBLISHER	FIRST PUBLISHED
	"The Four Suspects" from *The Thirteen Problems*	Collins Crime Club	1932
	Hallowe'en Party	Collins Crime Club	1969
	"The Herb of Death" from *The Thirteen Problems*	Collins Crime Club	1932
	Hickory Dickory Dock	Collins Crime Club	1955
	"How Does Your Garden Grow" from *The Regatta Mystery and Other Stories*	Dodd, Mead	1939
	The Mirror Crack'd from Side to Side	Collins Crime Club	1962
	Murder at the Vicarage	Collins Crime Club	1930
	The Mysterious Affair at Styles	John Lane The Bodley Head	1920
	Nemesis	Collins Crime Club	1971
	A Pocket Full of Rye	Collins Crime Club	1953
	Postern of Fate	Collins Crime Club	1973
	Sad Cypress	Collins Crime Club	1940
	Sleeping Murder	Collins Crime Club	1976
	They Do It With Mirrors	Dodd, Mead	1952
Collins, Wilkie	*The Moonstone*	Tinsley Brothers	1868
Connington, J. J.	*Murder in the Maze*	Ernest Benn	1927
Dickens, Charles	*The Mystery of Edwin Drood*	Chapman & Hall	1870
Dickinson, Peter	*The Yellow Room Conspiracy*	Mysterious Press	1994
Doyle, Arthur Conan	*A Study in Scarlet*	Ward, Lock	1887
	"Silver Blaze" (1892) in *The Memoirs of Sherlock Holmes*	George Newnes	1893
	"The Adventure of Wisteria Lodge" (1908) in *His Last Bow*	John Murray	1917
	"The Man with the Twisted Lip" (1891) from T*he Adventures of Sherlock Holmes*	George Newnes	1892

Book List

AUTHOR	TITLE	PUBLISHER	FIRST PUBLISHED
du Maurier, Daphne	*My Cousin Rachel*	Victor Gollancz	1951
Eglin, Anthony*	*The Blue Rose*	Dunne/Minotaur	2004
French, Tana	*The Wych Elm*	Penguin Viking	2018
Gazolli, Louise	*Compost Mortem*	Outskirts Press	2018
George, Elizabeth	*Missing Joseph*	Bantam Books	1993
Godden, Rumer	*An Episode of Sparrows*	Viking	1955
Grimes, Martha	*Jerusalem Inn*	Little, Brown	1984
Harris, Rosemary*	*Pushing Up Daisies*	CreateSpace	2014
Hawthorne, Nathaniel	"Rappaccini's Daughter" from *Mosses from an Old Manse*	Wiley & Putnam	1846
Hill, Reginald	*Deadheads*	Macmillan	1984
Hillerman, Tony	*The Wailing Wind*	HarperCollins	2002
Hirahara, Naomi*	*Gasa-Gasa Girl*	Bantam Dell	2005
	Strawberry Yellows	Prospect Park	2013
Hugg, Karen	*The Forgetting Flower*	Magnolia Press	2019
Humphreys, Helen	*The Lost Garden*	Norton	2002
Ironside, Elizabeth	*Death in the Garden*	Hodder & Stoughton	1995
James, P. D.	*An Unsuitable Job for a Woman*	Scribner	1973
Keene, Caroline	*Password to Larkspur Lane*	Grosset & Dunlap	1966
Khavari, Kate	*A Botanist's Guide to Parties and Poisons*	Crooked Lane Books	2022
Lane, Vicki*	*Signs in the Blood*	Bantam Dell	2005
MacLeod, Charlotte*	*Rest You Merry*	Mysterious Press	1978
	Trouble in the Brasses	Avon	1989
Marsh, Ngaio	*Grave Mistake*	Collins Crime Club	1978
McBride, James	*Deacon King Kong*	Riverhead	2020
Mills, Mark	*The Savage Garden*	Berkeley	2007
Orlean, Susan	*The Orchid Thief*	Random House	1988

AUTHOR	TITLE	PUBLISHER	FIRST PUBLISHED
Penny, Louise	*The Beautiful Mystery*	Minotaur	2012
	Trick of Light	Minotaur	2011
Perry, Anne	*A Sunless Sea*	Ballantine	2012
	Treachery at Lancaster Gate	Ballantine	2015
	Weighed in the Balance	Ballantine	1996
Peters, Ellis*	*Monk's Hood*	Morrow	1981
	A Morbid Taste for Bones	Morrow	1978
	One Corpse Too Many	Morrow	1980
Pim, Sheila	*Common or Garden Crime*	Hodder & Stoughton	1945
Pringle, Peter	*Day of the Dandelion*	Simon & Schuster	2007
Rabb, Margo	*Lucy Clark Will Not Apologize*	Quill Tree Books	2021
Rendell, Ruth	*The Crocodile Bird*	Crown	1993
	"Venus's Fly Trap" from *The Fallen Curtain*	Hutchinson	1976
	"Weeds" from *The Copper Peacock and Other Stories*	Mysterious Press	1991
Riggs, Cynthia*	*The Bee Balm Murders*	Minotaur	2011
	The Cranefly Orchid Murders	Dunne/Minotaur	2002
	Deadly Nightshade	Dunne/Minotaur	2001
Ripley, Ann*	*Mulch*	St. Martin's Press	1994
Rothenberg, Rebecca*	*The Bulrush Murders*	Carroll & Graaf	1991
Sayers, Dorothy L.	*Busman's Honeymoon*	Victor Gollancz	1937
	Strong Poison	Victor Gollancz	1930
	"Suspicion" from *In the Teeth of the Evidence*	Victor Gollancz	1939
	"The Fountain Plays" in *Hangman's Holiday*	Victor Gollancz	1933
	The Unpleasantness at the Bellona Club	Ernest Benn	1928
Shepherd, Lloyd	*The Poisoned Island*	Simon & Schuster UK	2013

AUTHOR	TITLE	PUBLISHER	FIRST PUBLISHED
Sherwood, John*	*The Mantrap Garden*	Scribner	1986
Stout, Rex*	*Black Orchids*	Farrar & Rinehart	1942
	Fer-de-Lance	Farrar & Rinehart	1934
	Murder by the Book	Viking Press	1951
Truman, Margaret	*Murder on Embassy Row*	Arbor House	1984
Walker, Martin*	*Bruno, Chief of Police*	Quercus	2008
Wan, Michelle*	*Deadly Slipper*	Doubleday	2005
Ware, Ruth	*Turn of the Key*	Harvill Secker	2019
Welty, Eudora	"A Curtain of Green" from *A Curtain of Green: A Book of Stories*	Doubleday	1941
Wentworth, Patricia	*The Gazebo*	J. B. Lippincott	1955
Whitney, Phyllis A.	*The Moonflower*	Fawcett	1958
Wingate, Marty*	*The Garden Plot*	Alibi (ebook only)	2014
Yu, Ovidia*	*The Mimosa Tree Mystery*	Constable	2020

Writer of plant- or garden-related mystery series.

SOURCES AND CITATIONS

EPIGRAPHS

"Gardening is not": Atwood, Margaret. "Unearthing Suite," *Bluebeard's Egg* (Toronto: McClelland and Stewart, 1983), 280.

"The vicar may": Sayers, Dorothy L. *Busman's Honeymoon* (1937). (New York: Avon Books, 1968), 193.

"It was ridiculous": Pim, Sheila. *Common or Garden Crime* (1945). (New York: Rue Morgue Press, 2001), 151.

"What lethal drops": Bradley, Alan. *The Sweetness at the Bottom of the Pie*. (New York: Delacorte Press, 2009), 152.

INTRODUCTION

"There is nothing": Doyle, Arthur Conan. "The Boscombe Valley Mystery" in *The Adventures of Sherlock Holmes* (New York: Barnes & Noble Books, 1995), 92.

For more on Poe's place in establishing the model for modern detective fiction see:

Martin, Terry J. "Detection, Imagination, and the Introduction to 'The Murders in the Rue Morgue.'" *Modern Language Studies*, vol. 19, no. 4 (Modern Language Studies, 1989), 31–45.

Grella, George. "Murder and Manners: The Formal Detective Novel," *NOVEL: A Forum on Fiction*, vol. 4, no. 1 (Duke University Press, 1970), 30–48.

GARDENING DETECTIVES, CLASSIC TO CONTEMPORARY

"One of these days": Collins, Wilkie. *The Moonstone*. (New York: Harper & Brothers, 1868), 56.

"The Last Rose of Summer," poem by Thomas Moore, 1779–1852, available at poets.org.

"If half the": Collins. *The Moonstone*. 55.

"as sharp as" and "as yellow as": Collins. *The Moonstone*. 56.

"When I *have*" and "old English rose" and "the right exposure": Collins. *The Moonstone*. 56.

The argument between Begbie and Cuff about grafting the white moss rose appears in *The Moonstone*, 95.

"the jolly Dog-Rose": Hole, S. Reynolds. *A Book About Roses*. (London: Edward Arnold, 1896), 133. Available at biodiversitylibrary.org.

"whole round of" and "flower-shows": Collins. *The Moonstone*. 99.

"Through the trellis-work" and "great man's gardener" and "has found out":
    Collins. *The Moonstone*. 175.

"Gardening is good": Christie, Agatha. *Murder at the Vicarage* (1930). (New
    York: Signet, 2000), 13.

Clues to Jane Marple's gardening were sourced from the following books
    and short stories:

KNOWLEDGE OR SKILL	REFERENCED IN:
Language of flowers	"The Four Suspects"
Scent of *Heliotropium* 'Cherry Pie'	*Nemesis*
Identification of silver-fleece vine	*Nemesis*
Plant identification in general	"Greenshaw's Folly"
Groundsel as a weed	*They Do It With Mirrors*
Ground elder as a weed	*At Bertram's Hotel*
Bindweed as a weed	*Sleeping Murder*
High standards for pruning	*Nemesis*
Slug problems	*They Do It With Mirrors*
Dolly as gardening friend	*Sleeping Murder*
Dolly's pride in her irises	*Mirror Crack'd From Side to Side*
Homemade tansy tea	"The Thumbmark of St. Peter"
Homemade damson gin	*Murder at the Vicarage*
Homemade cowslip wine	*4:50 from Paddington*

"They had entered": Peters, Ellis. *One Corpse Too Many*. (New York: Myste-
    rious Press, 1994), 15.

"I draw a great deal": Cranch, Robbie. "Mystery in the Garden: Interview
    with Ellis Peters," *Mother Earth Living*, December 1, 1993. Available at
    motherearthliving.com.

The Cadfael chronicles that reference lavender, in publication date order
    are *One Corpse Too Many*, *The Leper of St. Giles*, *The Virgin in the Ice*,

The Heretic's Apprentice, and *The Potter's Field*. See: Talbot, Rob and Robin Whiteman. *Brother Cadfael's Herb Garden*, (New York: Little, Brown, 1996.)

"Spike lavender (spica)": Von Bingen, Hildegard. *Physica*, translated by Priscilla Throop. (Rochester, Vermont: Healing Arts Press, 1998), 22.

"Everything in life must": Stout, Rex. *Fer-de-Lance* (1934). (New York: Bantam Books, 2008), 38.

"Wolfe started on orchids": Rex Stout writing as Archie Goodwin, "Why Nero Wolfe Likes Orchids," *Life Magazine*, 15 September 1963. Available at nerowolfe.org.

Bishop, Michael. "Orchids in the Corpus," a complete listing of all orchids in the Nero Wolfe books, available at nerowolfe.org.

"When people ask": Albert, Susan Wittig. *Queen Anne's Lace*. (New York: Berkley Prime Crime, 2018), 14.

SETTING: GARDEN SCENES OF THE CRIME

For more on the origins of the paradise garden, see *The Islamic Garden*. MacDougall, Elisabeth B., and Richard Ettinghausen, editors. (Washington, DC: Dumbarton Oaks, Trustees for Harvard University, 1976).

The story of Cain and Abel may be found in Genesis 4:1–17, King James version.

Shakespeare's description of murder in the garden appears in Hamlet, Act I, Scene V:

Sleeping within my orchard,
My custom always in the afternoon,
Upon my secure hour thy uncle stole

With juice of cursed hebenon in a vial,
And in the porches of my ears did pour
The leperous distilment, whose effect
Holds such an enmity with blood of man

From The Project Gutenberg eBook of Hamlet, available at gutenberg.org.

"Somehow, he thought": Christie, Agatha. *Hallowe'en Party* (1969). (London: HarperCollins, 2011 Ulverscroft Edition), 137 and 138.

Hercule Poirot's obituary appeared in *The New York Times*, 6 August 1975, 1, 16.

Gertrude Jekyll references from *The Mantrap Garden* by John Sherwood (New York: Charles Scribner's Sons, 1986), include *Yucca gloriosa* and *Euphorbia wulfenii* paired with red hot pokers, 28; quote from *Colour in the Garden*, 31; *Rosa* "The Garland," 62.

"Mysterious beauty of": Jekyll, Gertrude. *Wood and Garden*. (London: Longmans, Green, and Company, 1901), 30.

"People will sometimes": Jekyll, Gertrude. *Colour in the Flower Garden*. (London: Country Life, 1908), 89 and 90.

"Attached to her": Keene, Carolyn. *Password to Larkspur Lane*. (New York: Grosset and Dunlap, 1966), 38.

"It *is* funny": Nicolson, Harold. *Diaries and Letters*, Vol. III, Nigel Nicolson, editor. (New York: Atheneum, 1966), 257.

"Living in squares and loving in triangles" is a quote often attributed to Dorothy Parker, an attribution disputed by internet sources. It is also the title of a 2015 book by Amy License about Vanessa Bell and Virginia Woolf.

"Autumn in felted": Sackville-West, Vita. *The Garden*. (London: Michael Joseph Limited, 1946).

"The thing about": Humphreys, Helen. *The Lost Garden*. (New York: W. W. Norton & Company, 2002), 182.

"Now Adam": A poem published in *Kew Guild*, 1941, 61, quoted in *Gardening Women: Their Stories from 1600 to the Present* by Catherine Horwood. (London: Virago, 2010), 327.

"Let there be Gardens" and "These ardent passions": Virgil, *The Georgics*, translated by L. P. Wilkinson. (New York: Penguin, 1982), 127; Book 4, 86–87 and 108–109.

"Having laid out": Mills, Mark. *The Savage Garden*. (New York: Berkeley, 2007), 75.

"That's when Hettie": McBride, James. *Deacon King Kong*. (New York: Riverhead Books, 2020), 290.

"So I was": Dickinson, Peter. *The Yellow Room Conspiracy*. (New York: The Mysterious Press, 1994), 1.

MOTIVE: GARDENING MADE ME DO IT

"The neatness of": Rendell, Ruth. "Weeds," from *The Copper Peacock and Other Stories*. (New York: The Mysterious Press, 1991), 131.

"It is necessary" and "more sneaking and": Burnett, Frances Hodgson. *In the Garden*. (New York: The Medici Society of America, 1925), 21.

"My warfare with": Warner, Charles Dudley. *My Summer in a Garden*. (Boston: James R. Osgood & Company, 1871), 102.

"It's just rather": Hill, Reginald. *Deadheads*. (New York: Macmillan, 1984), 134.

"Any fool would": Eglin, Anthony. *The Blue Rose*. (New York: St. Martin's Minotaur, 2004), 44.

For more information on plant patent number 1, *Rosa* 'New Dawn', see "Climbing Rose" from *A History of Intellectual Property in 50 Objects* by Brad Sherman; Claudy Op Den Kamp and Dan Hunter, editors. (Cambridge: Cambridge University Press, 2019), 185–192.

Darwin, Charles. *On the Various Contrivances by Which British and Foreign Orchids Are Fertilized by Insects.* (London: John Murray, 1862).

"The air was": Chandler, Raymond. *The Big Sleep.* (1939). (New York: Ballantine Books, 1972), 13.

"They are nasty": Chandler. *The Big Sleep*, 15.

"'I see,' said": Wan, Michelle. *Deadly Slipper.* (New York: Doubleday, 2005), 15.

"He avoided their": Hawthorne, Nathaniel. "Rappaccini's Daughter" from *Mosses from an Old Manse* (1846). (London: G. Routledge & Company, 1852), 60.

MEANS: DIAL M FOR MULCH

"someone poisoned her": Beaton, M. C. *Agatha Raisin and the Potted Gardener.* (New York: St. Martin's Press, 1994), 107.

M. C. Beaton's Blockeley, inspiration for the village where Agatha Raisin settled, was also the Cotswold shooting location for much of the BBC's *Father Brown* mysteries, starring Mark Williams.

"The prisoner": Sayers, Dorothy L. *Strong Poison* (1930). (New York: HarperCollins, 1995), 8.

"When had he": Sayers, Dorothy L. "Suspicion" from *In the Teeth of the Evidence and Other Mysteries* (1940). (New York: Harper & Row, 1968), 183.

"Her eyes rested": Ripley, Ann. *Mulch.* (New York: St. Martin's Press, 1994), 137.

"She vomited": Ripley. *Mulch*, 61.

"Emma stared": Atherton, Nancy. *Aunt Dimity and the Duke.* (New York: Penguin, 1995), 51.

"The piece that killed": Aird, Catherine. *Passing Strange.* (Garden City, New York: Doubleday, 1981), 164.

"For Banks": Shepherd, Lloyd. *The Poisoned Island.* (London: Simon & Schuster, 2013), 25.

"*Contra vim mortis, nos est medicament in hortis*" is attributed to *Regimen sanitatis Salerni*, a health regimen written at the University of Salerno, then the Schola Medica Salernitana, possibly as far back as the tenth century. It was widely published during the Early Modern Period and has continued to be quoted regularly since then, for example in *Medical Botany, Vol. I*, by William Woodville. (London: James Phillips, 1790), 111.

Watson comments on Holmes's knowledge of botany and specific poisons in *A Study in Scarlet* by Arthur Conan Doyle. Doyle wrote "Gelsemium as a Poison" for *The British Medical Journal*, 20 September 1879, 483. Available at www.arthur-conan-doyle.com. Note, Agatha Christie also employed *Gelsemium* in a Poirot short story, "The Yellow Jasmine Mystery," published in magazine form in February 1924 and in book form as part of *The Big Four* (1927).

"It would not": George, Elizabeth. *Missing Joseph*. (New York: Bantam, 1993), 248.

The alkaloid toxin in *Conium* is called coniine. It acts as a paralytic and is also found in the pitcher plant (*Sarracenia flava*).

Midsomer Murders "Garden of Death" (Season 4, Episode 1) first aired in September 2000.

For more on Japanese strawberry farming in California's Pajaro Valley, see *Nihon Bunka/Japanese Culture: One Hundred Years in the Pajaro Valley* by Jane W. Borg and Kathy McKenzie Nichols. (Pajaro Valley Arts Council, 1992.) Available on the Santa Cruz [California] Public Library's local history site.

CLUES: GREEN EVIDENCE OR RED HERRINGS

"The reader must": Van Dine, S. S. "Twenty Rules for Writing Detective Stories," in *American Magazine*, September 1928. Reprinted in *Writing Suspense and Mystery Fiction*. A. S. Burack, editor. (Boston: The Writer, 1977), 267–272. Available at archive.org.

"We know in": P. D. James interview with Terry Gross, *Fresh Air*, 1 December 2014. Available at freshairarchive.org.

Wandersee, James H., and Elisabeth E. Schussler. "Preventing Plant Blindness," *The American Biology Teacher* 61, no. 2, 1999, 82–86.

"It's in the fall": Lane, Vicki. *Signs in the Blood*. (New York: Bantam Dell, 2005), 112.

"I think it's": Stasio, Marilyn. "Tony Hillerman, Novelist, Dies at 83," *The New York Times*, 27 October 2008.

"He rhapsodized": Rothenberg, Rebecca. *The Bulrush Murders*, (New York: Carroll & Graf, 1991), 62.

"*Helleborus niger*, the": Grimes, Martha. *Jerusalem Inn*. (New York: Little, Brown, 1984), 264.

"It was the first": Godden, Rumer. Quoted in the introduction to *An Episode of Sparrows*. (New York: New York Review of Books, 1955), xi.

SUSPECTS: SHADOWY GARDENERS

"Beyond, sheep were": Ironside, Elizabeth. *Death in the Garden*. (New York: Felony & Mayhem, 2005), 152.

For more information on Elizabeth Ironside, listen to her interview with Diane Rehm, 2 December 2005, available at dianerehm.org/shows.

"In the summer": Rendell, Ruth. *The Crocodile Bird*. (London: Hutchinson, 1993), 119.

"Verity read": Marsh, Ngaio. *Grave Mistake*. (Boston: Little, Brown, 1978), 44–45.

"Planting a garden": Constantine, K. C. *The Man Who Liked Slow Tomatoes*. (Boston: David R. Godine, 1982), 109.

"The garden, at any": Sayers, Dorothy L. *Busman's Honeymoon* (1937). (New York: Avon Books, 1968), 65.

"three circular garden", "heavy, hairy", "hanging up": Chesterton, G. K. "The Perishing of the Pendragons," from *The Wisdom of Father Brown* (1914). (New York: Penguin, 1970), 129.

MYSTERY WRITERS AND THEIR GARDENS: THE POISONED PEN—AND TROWEL

"An engagement to": Letter from Nathaniel Hawthorne to George S. Hillard, 16 July 1841, from *Selected Letters of Nathaniel Hawthorne*, Joel Myerson editor. (Columbus, Ohio: Ohio State University Press, 2002), 88.

"However rich" quoted in *Sophia Peabody Hawthorne, Volume I*, by Patricia Dunlavy Valenti. (Columbia, Missouri: University of Missouri Press, 2004), 14.

"too dull", "as to Lawyers", "becoming an Author": Nathaniel Hawthorne to Elizabeth Clarke Manning Hawthorne, 13 March 1821, quoted in *Nathaniel Hawthorne* by George Edward Woodberry. (Boston: Houghton Mifflin, 1902), 15–16.

"A man's soul": Nathaniel Hawthorne to Sophia Peabody 1 June 1841, quoted in *Passages from the American Note-books* by Nathaniel Hawthorne, Sophia Peabody Hawthorne, editor (1868). (Boston: Houghton Mifflin, 1886), 235.

"Burns never made": Hawthorne, Nathaniel. *The Blithedale Romance*. (Boston: Ticknor and Fields, 1855), 60.

"from the mere": Hawthorne, Nathaniel. *Mosses From an Old Manse*. (New York: George P. Putnam, 1851), 10.

"as red as" and "planted vegetables enough": Nathaniel Hawthorne to Zachariah Burchmore, quoted in *Hawthorne: A Life* by Brenda Wineapple. (New York: Random House, 2003), 220.

"of wide circumference": Hawthorne, Nathaniel. *The House of the Seven Gables* (1851). (New York: Charles E. Merrill, 1907) 33; "aristocratic flowers" and "plebian vegetables," 135; "wilderness of neglect", 125.

"The summer is not": Hawthorne. *Passages from the American Note-Books*, xxiv.

"Romance and poetry": Hawthorne, Nathaniel. *The Marble Faun* (1859). (Akron, Ohio: Saalfield Publishing, 1902), iv.

"Perhaps if we": Hawthorne, Nathaniel. *Complete Works, vol. 9*. (Boston: Houghton Mifflin, 1883), 393.

"The garden was" and "excitingly tall": Christie, Agatha. *An Autobiography*. (New York: Dodd, Mead, 1977), 9.

"the bedroom slops, my dear. Liquid manure–nothing like it!": Christie. *An Autobiography*. 29.

"our children": Thompson, Laura. *Agatha Christie: A Mysterious Life*. (London: Pegasus Books. Kindle Edition, 2018), 345.

"a beautiful jungle,": Christie. *An Autobiography*, 495.

"Hitler-Lavin": Thompson. *Agatha Christie: A Mysterious Life*, 423.

"the loveliest place" Agatha Christie to Max Mallowan, 27 October 1942 quoted in *Agatha Christie: A Mysterious Life* by Thompson. 310.

The 80th birthday article on Rex Stout's irises: "Rex Stout Marks 80th Year With New Book," by Marian P. Prilock in *The Owasso [Michigan] Argus-Press* (AP). December 1, 1966, 29.

On Ruth Stout, see "More Vegetables, Less Work: Lessons from the Mother of Mulch," by Barbara Damrosch in *The Washington Post*, March 9, 2017.

"And *you* turning": Stout, Ruth. "Verdict: Iris are Wonderful," *Popular Gardening*. June 1956, 48–53, available at nerowolfe.org.

"I write for 39" and "I figure on six": Whitman, Alden. "Rex Stout, Creator of Nero Wolfe, Dead." *The New York Times*, October 29, 1975. 1, 36.

"The bee balm": Riggs, Cynthia. *The Bee Balm Murders*. (New York: Minotaur Books, 2011), 1.

IMAGE CREDITS

Illustrations by Yolanda V. Fundora unless noted below.

Page 21 Image of Sgt. Cuff, Courtesy of the University of St Andrews
Libraries and Museums, Ref. Har PR4494.M7 1894

Page 63, The Gazebo, Courtesy of the author. The Gazebo: A Miss Silver
Mystery by Patricia Wentworth

Page 101, Arthur Conan Doyle, Library of Congress. Bain News Service.
#LC-DIG-ggbain-12334

Page 161, Agatha Christie, Popperfoto via Getty Images

Page 162, Greenway, Popperfoto via Getty Images

Page 164, Rex Stout, Courtesy of the author

Page 165, Black Orchids, Courtesy of the author. Black Orchids: A
Nerowolfe Double Mystery by Rex Stout

Page 166, Karen Hugg, R. Hope Hugg

Page 170 and 171, Vicki Lane and garden, Vicki Lane

Page 175, Cynthia Riggs, Lynn Christoffers

Page 177, Naomi Hirahara, Mayumi Hirahara

ACKNOWLEDGMENTS

To Pamela Zave, Sandra Swan, Linda O'Gorman, and Thelma Achenbach for commenting on the manuscript in draft, and to Stephen R. Johnson, PhD, toxicologist, for your review of the chapter on plant poisons. Remaining errors are mine alone.

To David Wheeler, editor of *Hortus*, who has encouraged many of my pen-and-trowel wanderings, including "The Verdant Letters: Hawthorne and Horticulture" (Summer 2004).

To librarians hither and yon, especially the marvelous staff of the Library of the Chathams and The New York Botanical Garden's LuEsther T. Mertz Library.

To the mystery lovers who offered leads on additional titles, notably Judy Glattstein, Sally Hemsen, Becky Hoskins, Chris Schorr, and Fran Ziegler at Titcomb's Bookshop.

To Lucia Mastronardi and Leah O'Gorman for the Harry Potter expertise.

To Dr. Carolyn Rehm, for the discussion on digitalis therapies in treating heart patients.

To Amy Stewart. Though my hopes were dashed on horticultural references in your *Kopp Sisters* series, thank you for the tip on Naomi Hirahara.

To Martin Stott, for the information on Samuel Reynolds Hole.

To mystery devotees who, over time, have shared their expertise in a variety of media, especially The Dorothy L. Sayers Society, The Wolfe Pack, and contributors to fanwikis for Agatha Christie, Baker Street, and *Midsommer Murders*.

To investigators of Dame Agatha who came before:

Kathryn Harkup, *A is for Arsenic: The Poisons of Agatha Christie* (2015)

Anne Hart, *The Life and Times of Miss Jane Marple* (1985)

Joyce H. Newman, *Agatha Christie's Gardens* (2020)

To Vicki Lane, Naomi Hirahara, Karen Hugg, Cynthia Riggs, and Ruth Ware for your generous answers to my queries. And to all the other amazing writers of crime fiction, please let me know if you garden.

INDEX

de Luce, Flavia, 102, 112
De Quincey, Thomas, 108
detective fiction, 13–15
Dickens, Charles, 17, 108
Dickinson, Peter, 62, 64
Digitalis purpurea, 111–112
Dionaea muscipula, 103
Divine Comedy (Dante), 58, 83
Docci, Federico, 58–59
Dogger, Arthur Wesley, 41
Doyle, Arthur Conan, 99–101, 107–108
Drew, Nancy, 49–51
du Maurier, Daphne, 118
Dunn, Bedie, 79–80
Dunn, Mara, 79–80
Dupin, Chevalier C. Auguste, 14

E

Earle, Alice Morse, 39
Eglin, Anthony, 75–77
Eldridge, Louise, 94–95
Emerson, Ralph Waldo, 155
Endeavour, HMS, 103, 105
English Physician of 1652, The (Culpeper), 33
Episode of Sparrows, An (Godden), 132–133
Equal Rights Amendment (1971), 94
Euphorbia marginata, 122
Euphorbia wulfenii, 47

F

Fallopia aubertii, 26
Farnese, Vincino, 60
Fer-de-Lance (Stout), 33, 36, 166
Five Little Pigs (Christie), 163
Flesh of the Orchid, The (Chase), 78

Flintwine, Jeremy, 68–70
floral wire, 97
"Flowers of the Strange Orchid, The" (Wells), 103
forensic botany, 125–126
Forgetting Flower, The (Hugg), 105–106, 168
Fortune, Mary, 90–91
Foster, Sybil, 144
"Fountain Plays, The" (Sayers), 148
fountains, 148
4:40 from Paddington (Christie), 114
foxglove, 85, 111–112
Franklin, Benjamin, 116
French, Tana, 64, 168
Furmidable Foes (Brown), 118

G

Gaboriau, Emile, 15
Gamache, Armond, 65
Gardener, Bruce, 143–144
Gardening Illustrated (periodical), 51
Garden Murder Case, The (Van Dine), 121
Garden Plot, The (Wingate), 64
garden tools, as means, 93–97
Gasa-Gasa Girl (Hirahara), 133–135, 178
Gazebo, The (Wentworth), 63, 64
Gazzoli, Louise, 74
Gelsemium sempervirens, 100
Genesis, Book of, 43
Genus Rosa, The (Willmott), 55
George, Elizabeth, 110
Georgics (Virgil), 57
Geraghty, Mike, 94
Gibbons, Marion Chesney, 89
ginseng, 124–125

Mason, Lovejoy, 132–133

mazes, 64

McBride, Angus, 143

McBride, James, 60–62

Melville, Herman, 156

memento mori gardens, 58–59

Merchant of Venice, The (Shakespeare), 74

Metamorphoses (Ovid), 58

Midnight in the Garden of Good and Evil
    (Berendt), 44

Midsomer Murders (television series), 115

Miller, Frederick, 159

Miller, Madge, 158

Miller, Margaret, 159

Mills, Mark, 57–60

Mimosa Tree Mystery, The (Yu), 97

Mirror Crack'd from Side to Side, The
    (Christie), 27–28

Missing Joseph (George), 110

Molière, 57

monkshood, 114–115

Monk's Hood (Peters), 115

Monty Miller, 158

Moonflower, The (Whitney), 12

moonflowers, 12, 61

Moonstone, The (Collins), 17–24, 181

Moore, Thomas, 18–24

Morbid Taste for Bones, A (Peters), 31

Mosses from an Old Manse (Hawthorne), 156

moss-rose, 70

Mother Earth Living (periodical), 31

Mulch (Ripley), 94–95

Mummery, Harold, 92–93

Murder at the Vicarage (Christie), 24–25

Murder by the Book (Stout), 36

Murder in Retrospect (Christie), 163

Murder in the Maze (Connington), 64

Murder Most Florid (Spencer), 125

murder mystery structure, 13

Murder of Roger Ackroyd, The (Christie), 44

Murder on Embassy Row (Truman), 113

Murder on the Red River (Rendon), 116

"Murders in the Rue Morge" (Poe), 14

My Cousin Rachel (du Maurier), 118

Mysterious Affair at Styles, The (Christie),
    108, 160

Mystery of Edwin Drood, The (Dickens), 108

My Summer in a Garden (Warner), 70

N

Nancy Drew series, 11, 49–50

National Public Radio, 122

Navajo culture, 126–127

Nemesis (Christie), 28

New York Botanical Garden, 110

New York Times (periodical), 45

Nicolson, Harold, 51

Noakes, Mr., 146–147

No Orchids for Miss Blandish (Chase), 77–78

O

Old Time Gardens (Earle), 39

Oliver, Ariadne, 45

One Corpse Too Many (Peters), 29

On the Various Contrivances by Which British
    and Foreign Orchids are Fertilized by
    Insects (Darwin), 77

opioids, 107–108

opium poppy, 32, 106–109

orchids, 33, 34–37, 77–81

Orchid Thief, The (Orlean), 77

Orchis mascula, 33

Index

Index